AMAZING TEXAS

Fascinating Facts, Entertaining Tales, Bizarre
Happenings, and Historical Oddities About the
Lone Star State

By T. Jensen Lacey

ISBN: 978-0977808694
Library of Congress Control Number: 2008929432

Cover design by Jerry Dorris
Interior design by David Jones Gallery
First Printing July 2008

Printed in the United States

Published by Jefferson Press

jefferson press

P.O. Box 115
Lookout Mountain, TN 37350

TABLE OF CONTENTS

Foreword
Preface
Acknowledgments

Dedication

To my dad, Houston-born Joseph James Jensen (October 10, 1917–September 26, 2004), a true Texan if ever there was one, and to my maternal grandmother, another devout Texan (born in Blue Ridge), Simmie Catherine Parker Bagwell (May 12, 1903–February 10, 1986), who taught me everything there is to know about appreciating faith, family, and one's roots.

Acknowledgments

First, my family members: thanks to my mom, Marian Bagwell Jensen, for being my navigator, research assistant, and proofreader, and for being there for me (as always); to my husband, Eric, for helping proofread the text (and giving me space and peace to write); to my father-in-law and attorney extraordinaire, Richard C. Lacey Sr., for his help with the book contract and for going over the manuscript with a fine-tooth comb; to my sister Patricia Jensen Edmundson for her tireless research and fabulous finds; to Paige Ward Estigarribia for her research and eye for those good stories; and to Paige's baby, Isabelle, who was gracious enough to sleep and allow Mom to work!

Thanks also to the Texas Historical Commission—the list of all the items they helped me with would make a book on its own and to Ken Biggs with Lone Star Internet, Inc., for his help with famous (and infamous) Texans; the staff of Handbook of Texas Online for being available for all my questions; to Sarah Gerichten and Mary Boyer of Bat Conservation International, for their help with my bat tales; to official Texas Chainsaw Massacre Fan Club President Tim Harden for his time and for information about film sites around Austin; and to Christy Marino at the Spindletop/Gladys City Boomtown for permission to use the photo of the Lucas Gusher (and thanks to Myrtle Locke at their Museum for the interview).

Thanks to Jim Willett for his photographs of and stories about the Texas State Prison, the museum by the same name, the prison rodeo, and cemetery stories. Thanks to Andrew Suber of the Alpine Chamber of Commerce for information on the annual Texas Cowboy Poetry Gathering. To Jennifer Nalewicki with the Texas Department of Transportation, you were a huge help in so many ways and a great resource for me. Thanks to Alfred Shepperd for the Stonehenge II story and to Doug and Shaleah Hill for the photos. Thanks also to Jessica Harris of the Dr Pepper Museum for being so helpful. The staff of National Geographic magazine were also quite helpful in my attempts to find archived articles relating to Texas.

A big thanks goes to the staff of TexasEscapes.com, especially editor John Troesser, columnist Mike Cox, historian Bob Bowman, and "outlaw specialist" Charley Eckhardt, for help, photos, and access to archived articles (www. texasescapes.com). Thanks to Rena and Sammy Andrews, owners of Andrews Ranch, for the story on Bodacious, the "World's Most Dangerous Bull," and to the docents of the O. Henry Museum in Austin for additional background on the museum. Gil Glover of Dallas View was most helpful with stories concerning the area, and Don Elefante, thanks for looking over what I wrote about the Eckankar religion. Thanks to Hazel Gully of Sanderson, Texas, for the cactus recipe and the photo of Raylene, the Cactus Queen. For the story on and photo of the sub chasers, a big thanks goes to the Texas Maritime Museum in Rockport. To the staff of the Forbidden Gardens in Katy, thanks for your patience and providing me with great pictures.

To my godmother, San Antonio native Alice Romero, and to Austinian Jacci Howard Bear, thanks for the recipes and information on the "Big Three" dishes in Texas.

A special thanks goes to Governor Rick Perry and his press assistant, Catherine Blackburn Frazier, for their time and for graciously writing the text for the back cover for Amazing Texas.

TRULY BIZARRE EVENTS, UNEXPLAINED PHENOMENA, AND NOTORIOUS TEXANS

Bonnie Parker: "The Legend of Bonnie and Clyde"

Some movie makers have romanticized the legendary robber couple of Bonnie Parker and Clyde Barrow, but not my family: She was one of us - a distant cousin to me - although her name went unmentioned at family reunions. Born in Rowena, Texas, in 1910, Bonnie led a tragic, brief life because of the choices she made.

Her father was a bricklayer and died when Bonnie was only 4 years old. Her mother, Emma, moved with the three children—big brother Hubert, Bonnie, and younger sister Billie, to the West Dallas community dubbed Cement City. An above-average student in school, Bonnie was unfortunately drawn to bad-guy types; she married young to a man named Roy Thornton, who was later sentenced to prison.

It was after this that 19-year-old Bonnie met the soon-to-be-notorious Clyde Barrow, who also was a ne'er-do-well, jailed shortly after he and Bonnie met. Once he was paroled, he and Bonnie began terrorizing the South, robbing banks, stealing cars, and writing letters to the newspapers, taunting the police they were eluding.

Joining them on their murderous rampages throughout Texas, Missouri, New Mexico, and Oklahoma were Barrow's brother, Buck, and his wife, Blanche. When the gang began to routinely kill police officers in their rampages, the authorities doubled their efforts to bring an end to the Parker-and-Barrow reign of terror. Finally, they were able to kill Buck and capture Blanche.

It was a beautiful day in May 1934 when Bonnie and Clyde met their violent fate. They were riding along a quiet country road when officers ambushed them at Black Lake, Louisiana. The shooting lasted a full minute—with bullets flying through the car—and the legendary couple's wild ride was over. Both bodies were displayed in Dallas before they were placed in their families' burial sites.

Today you can see their graves in Dallas. Clyde and his brother Buck are buried in Western Heights Cemetery; Bonnie is in Crown Hill Memorial Park. Her epitaph is ironic, considering how she led her life:

Tombstone of Bonnie Parker. Courtesy findagrave.com.

As the flowers are made sweeter by The sunshine and the dew, so this old World is made brighter by the lives Of folks like you.

A "Royal" Murder Mystery

The city of Fort Stockton, with a current population of a little more than 7,500, claims among its residents descendants of those tough pioneers often referred to as settlers. Sometimes those settlers took matters into their own rawhide-tough hands when they were displeased.

One person who displeased a lot of settlers was A.J. Royal, sheriff of Pecos County in the late 1880s. He presided over all legal matters from his desk in the courthouse.

Some of the townspeople—said to be a half dozen or so businessmen with grudges against Sheriff Royal—apparently drew straws to determine who would send the sheriff to the great "courthouse in the sky." The election of 1894 was coming up, tensions were high, and the Texas Rangers had come to town to keep a lid on the increasingly volatile atmosphere.

Sheriff Royal was not reelected and two weeks later was mysteriously murdered at his desk. No one was ever accused of the crime, and although the Rangers were still in town, no one was ever arrested on suspicion of murder. Suddenly, it seemed no one in this small, close-knit community knew anything.

One of the town's settlers was Annie Riggs, who came to town in 1877 and built a hotel in 1899. Riggs is of course long gone, but she left behind a legacy in the form of the Annie Riggs Hotel Museum. The museum houses all kinds of cowboy and Native American artifacts—but there is one eerie item that still has bloodstains on it—the desk of Sheriff A.J. Royal, mysteriously murdered in 1894.

Although your kids might enjoy touring the Cowboy Room or seeing tusks of a Columbian mammoth on the premises, the desk is what intrigues most adults.

The museum is located on South Main Street, and admission is free.

Leapin' Lizards! (or, the Amazing Story of Old Rip)

In the town of Eastland (the seat of Eastland County) in 1897, the townspeople built their courthouse. That in itself isn't unusual, but what they added to the cornerstone was.

According to local lore, the justice of the peace put a small horned toad in a hole they made in the cornerstone for the (live) toad's resting place. The toad's name was Old Rip.

In 1928, a new courthouse was built, but before the old courthouse was razed, the townspeople gathered to see the original cornerstone reopened. Inside was Old Rip, who at first appeared dead, but when someone touched the toad, he leapt to life.

His miraculous resurrection made national news, and he was taken on a tour of the country. They say that he lived until 1929, when he died of pneumonia. The horned toad is the state reptile, and this story is a beloved one among Texans. Incidentally, the courthouse has Old Rip on display in a glass-front casket, if you want to go pay your respects. The city also hosts Old Ripfest on the third Saturday of every September.

Texas's Pirate

The city of Galveston is named in honor of the Count of Galvez in Spain, Bernardo de Gálvez y Madrid, but more people are familiar with the history of the infamous pirate, Jean Lafitte, who struck terror in the hearts of nineteenth-century Texans. Born around 1780 in France, once in the United States, Jean and his brother Pierre began a smuggling operation, for a time living in and working out of New Orleans. In an attempt to sway the U.S. government's feelings toward them and their way of life, the brothers even sided with American forces, helping Andrew Jackson win the Battle of New Orleans in 1815.

Their efforts went unappreciated by President James Madison, however, and Jean and Pierre continued their illicit activities. A fellow pirate, Louis-Michel Aury, established a European settlement in the Galveston area as his base of operations in support of Mexico's rebellion against Spanish rule. Jean Lafitte took over it in 1817 during Aury's absence. The Lafitte brothers needed a base of operations of their own because they had just been driven from their base at Barataria Bay, Louisiana.

Jean Lafitte made the island of Galveston into a haven for pirates, with himself the head of its informal government. Finally, in May 1820, the U.S. Navy gave the brothers an ultimatum: leave Galveston or be annihilated. Jean burned the settlement, but it is rumored that he left the bulk of his treasure in the area, planning to return.

Author Harris Gaylord Warren has written that Jean Lafitte died off the coast of Yucatan around 1825. Many say Lafitte's treasure is still hidden somewhere on Galveston Island.

The Ghost Capital of Texas

The spooky title of Ghost Capital of Texas belongs to Old Town Spring, north-west of Houston. Tour guide Randy Woods says to bring your camera. He tells me that you are virtually guaranteed a ghost sighting because this area of the state has had more ghost sightings and unex-plainable eerie phenomena than in any other part of Tex-as, period. See the "Virtual Texas" section near the end of this book for his Web site ad-dress.

Ghost Capital of Texas. Courtesy Randy Woods.

Kids Getting Antsy?

If your kids are bored, you might want to take them by the Sabine County Jail in Hemphill. In this four-celled jail is a gallows that is nearly 100 years old. If you can't get there, take the tykes to see Old Sparky in the Texas Prison

Museum. It was the state's electric chair between 1924 and 1964.

The sight of either of these just might give them pause—and you relief, at least for a little while.

Strange But True!

Historical Outhouse

The city of Henderson, Texas, has as one of its claims to fame the only outhouse in the state with its own historical marker. It's a quite ornate building—a three-holer to boot!—and was originally built for an eminent lawyer in town. Check out the gingerbread décor, but you can't use this facility for its original intent. Nowadays, it's for entertainment purposes only.

The Most Bizarre and Notorious of All

Weather may not, at first blush, appear to be appropriate for this chapter, but no one person or event has killed more people in Texas than this unpredictable force. The great hurricane of 1900 claimed more than 6,000 lives in Galveston. You can learn more about it through the multi-image presentation that shows on the hour at Pier 21 in there.

More than three fourths of the city of Indianola was devastated by a hurricane in 1875; although the people who survived struggled to rebuild their town, another hurricane struck in 1886, destroying what remained of the town. Today, a handful of anglers make the area their home, and other than a historical marker and a statue dedicated to French explorer René-Robert Cavelier, Sieur de La Salle, there is little to remind visitors that Indianola used to be a bustling, prosperous town.

People who live in the path of hurricanes have

learned to work together for the mutual good. I refer to this as hurricane culture. (For more information on hurricanes and hurricane culture, see Chapter 14, "Lighthouse and Costal Stories.")

Give 'Em a Big Hand . . . Er, Foot

In 1994 a man named Craig Woolheater and his wife were driving late at night and saw what they believed to be Bigfoot. Woolheater became obsessed with the creature, who is also known as Woolly Booger in Texas. Since seeing the creature, Woolheater has discovered that Bigfoot sightings aren't relegated to just the Pacific Northwest: Bigfoot has been reported in every state but Hawaii, he says.

Now Woolheater is director of the Texas Bigfoot Research Center near Dallas, which has its own Web site. Although there is no official statement forthcoming from the Texas Parks and Wildlife Department as to whether or not the creature exists, Woolheater's research center has gathered more than 100 claims of sightings from all over the Lone Star State, submitted to the center's Web site.

Hotfoot it to the "Virtual Texas" section near the back of this book for that!

The Country's Oldest Bank Robber

The town of Lubbock, Texas, was where probably the oldest person ever to rob a bank in this country was sentenced. In January 2004, 91-year-old J.L. "Red" Hunter Rountree was sentenced to 12 years in prison for bank robbery.

Rountree had robbed banks in other states—Mississippi and Florida—and had served time for only some of his crimes. Florida gave him three years' prison time; Mississippi, only three years' probation. My guess is that because he was 87 when he robbed a bank in Biloxi, Mississippi, he was given a light sentence because of his advanced age.

CNN quoted Rountree as saying to the Orlando Sentinel that the food was better in prison than in nursing homes and that he was robbing banks as a way to get back at them because he felt that he'd been forced into bankruptcy by a bank in Corpus Christi, Texas.

When I was trying to locate Rountree for an interview, I discovered that he'd died in prison, on October 12, 2004, at the U.S. Medical Center for Federal Prisoners in Springfield, Missouri. One source said that his body was unclaimed and that he was buried on the prison grounds. By the time this book went to press, no family member had been located to let me know otherwise.

It'll Bug You Forever If You Don't Visit This Museum

It all started with a contest to find the best-dressed roach in the country. An exterminator, Michael "Cockroach Dundee" Bohdan, was contest overseer for Combat brand roach bait and traveled throughout the United Stated in the 1980s. (In 1986 he was a guest on the Tonight Show, with Dallas's largest cockroach—it was 1.88 inches long).

"When the contest was over, they [the company] were going to throw [the roaches] away, and I decided to just take 'em and see what I could do with them," Bohdan told me. Bohdan created an exhibit of the winners. The roaches are now on display in Plano, Texas, at the Cockroach Hall of Fame Museum on 15th Street, which Bohdan runs. Some of the exhibits include Liberoachi, who wears a white cape and sits at a tiny piano, and Marilyn Monroach. There's even a salute to the movie Psycho, with a tiny Combates Motel and a dagger-wielding roach on the diminutive premises. Approximately 6,000 people tour the museum annually, and a shop on the premises sells

T-shirts and coffee mugs bearing the Cockroach Hall of Fame Museum logo.

"I've written a book entitled <u>What's Bugging You?</u> [It's] a do-it-yourself book for people who want to do their own exterminating," Bohdan told me. "I will have ten to fifteen people a day come in with bags of bugs for me to identify, and they sometimes bring me a roach, dressed for the museum."

The Santa Claus Bank Robbery

It was two days before Christmas in the year 1927 that the infamous Santa Claus Bank Robbery stunned the state of Texas and the nation. With the oil boom still going on and the Great Depression yet to come, many Texans were making their fortunes. It wasn't only law-abiding citizens making their fortunes, though; so was the criminal element. On average, it was common on a daily basis for several banks in the state to be robbed.

In desperation, the Texas Bankers Association offered a reward: Anyone shooting a bank robber in the midst of the crime would be paid $5,000. Suddenly, the law-abiding citizens of Texas perceived that becoming a vigilante might put money in their pockets.

On December 23, 1927, ex-convict Marshall Ratliff joined forces with two other ex-cons, Henry Helms and Robert Hill, intending to rob the First National Bank in Cisco. They were joined by Helms's relative, Louis Davis. They arrived from Wichita Falls, where they had been staying at a boardinghouse owned by a woman named Midge Tellet. As they approached the bank, Ratliff added a holiday touch to their attempt—he put on a Santa Claus outfit that he had borrowed from Mrs. Tellet.

Into the bank the trio went, but not before they were spotted by some children outside the bank. The children began following the men—they were with Santa Claus, after all—and this attracted attention to the group. As the robbers entered the bank, one customer saw them from outside and began screaming for help, saying a robbery attempt was underway inside. Her screams were heard by Chief of Police G.E. Bedford, and he, along with some armed citizens, entered the bank. In an exchange of gunfire, several people were wounded, including Alex Spears, the bank president.

Two of the children—two small girls—were taken hostage as the four men attempted their getaway, and in the alley, there was another exchange of gunfire. In this one, Chief Bedford and a deputy were both mortally wounded, as were Ratliff and Davis.

One thing the robbers hadn't planned on was needing gas, but they realized two things as they attempted escape: Their car was low on fuel, and it had a tire shot out. Pursued by vigilantes and police alike, they commandeered another car and wound up in another exchange of gunfire. This time, Hill was wounded. Leaving the wounded Davis in the commandeered car, which had no keys, they returned to their original car but inadvertently left their booty with Davis.

The pursuers found Davis and the money and returned the latter to the bank—more than $12,000 had been taken. Witnesses said that there were hundreds of bullet holes in the building. At that point, six people had been wounded, including the police officers. Davis died within hours of being taken into custody, at a nearby hospital.

Leaving their car and their little hostages outside town, the robbers stole another car and wrecked it in another town nearby, whereby they commandeered another vehicle. They had the driver of the car drive them for approximately a day, then set him free after stealing another vehicle.

The situation of the three wounded robbers was getting ever more desperate—they were hungry and tired, and it was bitterly cold. When they attempted to cross the Brazos River, they were set upon by a sheriff. Another car pursuit was on.

They made one final attempt at freedom in a shoot-out. It is a popular story that the one man to end the men's flight was a Texas Ranger by the name of Cy Bradford, who, it is said, shot all three men.

In the end, all of them faced justice. Hill was sentenced to 99 years in prison. He was paroled in the mid-1940s and finally became a law-abiding citizen. Helms was sentenced to death in the electric chair in September 1929. Ratliff was sentenced to execution and pleaded insanity. While his plea was being considered, he killed a guard in an escape attempt.

The people of the town had had enough: They hung Ratliff themselves on November 19, 1929. No one was ever tried for the crime of lynching.

You can still see the bank in Cisco, although it has been rebuilt. There is a painting depicting the robbery, and the Texas Historical Commission placed a historical marker on the site in 1967.

The Infamous Lincoln County War

Tempers flared into violence between two groups of men on the western frontier in 1878. One group included wealthy ranchers; the other, the owners of a general store with monopolistic tendencies in Lincoln County, New Mexico. Most of the men involved in the fighting were on the Texas side of the border. The violence began when the store owners claimed that one of the ranchers owed them money and they seized his horses in payment. When the rancher challenged this group of deputized men, he was killed. His friends were then deputized to capture the killers; you may have heard of them as "The Regulators."

By July, more than 20 men on both sides had been shot and killed, with even more wounded. When the Regulators shot at government troops, their fate was sealed.

This war served only to foster an abiding sense of distrust in the region and to make criminals out of the Regulators who survived. Those fugitives included a young Texan with a lust for violence, William H. Bonney, whom you might know even better as Billy the Kid.

You can see artifacts relating to Billy the Kid and the Lincoln County War at the Nita Stewart Haley Memorial Library and J. Evetts Haley History Center in Odessa. In the town of Hico, there is a Billy the Kid Museum.

The Ghost Tracks of San Antonio

On any night, and especially the night of Halloween, you might see cars lined up to pause on the train tracks that meet at Shane and Villamain roads. They're stopping there to test a legend.

The legend has it that back around 1940, a school bus carrying approximately a dozen children stalled on these very tracks, and all were killed when an oncoming train struck the bus. The legend further says that now, in an attempt to keep this from ever happening again, small, unseen hands push cars off the tracks if they are stopped there.

To see if this is true, some people have gone so far as to put talcum powder on their cars; they swear that after leaving the tracks, they can then see tiny hand- and fingerprints, made by invisible ghostly heroes.

La Grange: Known for Its Diverse Inhabitants, Huma. and Otherwise

Despite its beginnings as a humble buffalo trail, the city of La Grange has long been known for its diverse demographics. Many Czechoslovakians settled here; Czech settler Heinrich L. Kreische established one of the first commercial breweries in Texas here, which is still in operation.

There's something more, though, that attracts some people to this town: the ghosts of the former Fayette County jailhouse. Built in 1883, it was used as a jail until 1985. About 10 years later, the county chamber of commerce took over the building.

Many former inmates have made their malevolent presences known since then. One, whom locals refer to as the Widow Dach, has made visitors and employees alike more than a little uncomfortable. Jailed on the charge of murdering a farmworker, the widow is said to have gone on a hunger strike—and died.

Locals say everyone refuses to work there after dark, for many reasons. For example, hanging from the ceiling on the ground floor is a hangman's noose, now used for a conversation piece rather than for executions. Sometimes the noose begins to swing back and forth, as if moved by an unseen presence. Jailhouse employees have heard drawers slam and crashing sounds, with no evident cause. They also say that pictures are sometimes moved from their usual places on walls, and they sometimes even hear footsteps.

Go visit the La Grange Area Chamber of Commerce offices if you dare—but do it before sunset.

Royalty That Wasn't

The town of Mina changed its name to honor one of its residents, supposedly a man of royal Dutch blood named Felipe Enrique Neri, Baron de Bastrop. He arrived in Texas in 1805, and with his title as a banner before him, secured a grant for a colony, opened a freighting business, and was appointed second alcalde (a kind of judicial officer) of San Antonio in 1810.

Baron de Bastrop achieved eminence in other ways too: He was elected as a representative to the Mexican state of Coahuila, which at that time included Texas, and negotiated with the government of Mexico for Stephen F. Austin's original colony.

The baron died penniless, and townsfolk collected money for his burial. It was then they learned that the he was an imposter with a price on his head. He was wanted in Holland for embezzlement!

Tragedy in Texas City

Any farmer can tell you how explosive ammonium nitrate is. Can you imagine the terrible mayhem that a ship full of it would cause if it caught fire? The French cargo ship SS Grandcamp was a floating time bomb.

When the ship exploded in the Texas City port on the misty morning of April 16, 1947, it took everyone by surprise. The city was suddenly filled with casualties as firefighters and onlookers were burned or killed by flying debris. The situation got rapidly worse: A tidal wave, about 15 feet high, swept the dock area. Another ship carrying ammonium nitrate, the SS High Flyer, also caught fire and exploded about 16 hours later. However, the first explosion had killed 26 firefighters and destroyed virtually all of the city's firefighting equipment, leaving the city helpless in the wake of the second explosion.

The devastation left Texas City with approximately 580 people dead, 178 missing, and thousands of people injured. Damages to surrounding homes and the downtown area totaled about $68 million. Oil resources that went flaming into the night sky were valued at half a billion dollars (in 1947 figures), so it would be much more today. Thousands of people were left homeless due to the devastation from the explosions and fires. The unidentified dead were buried on June 22 in the city in a cemetery created for them, the Memorial Cemetery; no others have been buried there.

Today, the Texas City Museum honors the memory of those who died in the worst disaster in Texas history. The town has quite a number of things to see relating to the disaster. The Moore Memorial

Fighting fire on board ship during the 1947 Texas City Disaster. Unidentified photographer. Moore Memorial Public Library, Texas City.

Library has digitized photographs of the tragedy, the propeller of the Highflyer is located at the Texas City Terminal Railway, and Fire Station 2 has a plaque with the names of the 28 firefighters who died that day.

Because of the 1947 calamity, legislation created new safeguards for ships hauling such potentially dangerous chemicals.

Q & A

Q. What small village in Big Bend Country had an army post stationed there (circa 1915) to protect the area from Mexican bandit Pancho Villa?

A. Lajitas

Q. Who was the Naked Lady of Nacogdoches, a turn-of-the-eighteenth-century entertainer who rode horseback, wearing (they say) only a cloak as part of her act?

A. Adah Isaacs Menken

Q. What tough, notorious sheriff, who held office from 1932 through 1954 in Henderson County, earned his reputation by shooting a total of nine men (three fatally) during his tenure, including Gerald Johnson, known as the Dallas Kid?

A. Sheriff Jess Sweeten

Q. What city is home to Medical Plastics Laboratory, Inc., which produces anatomically correct human body parts and gives tours of its facility?

A. Gatesville

Q. What town contains the burial site of "Bloody Bill" Longley, who killed more than 32 men in his young life before being hanged in this town in 1878?

A. Giddings; there is a historical marker marking the spot in a small cemetery on U.S. Highway 290

Q. Why did Ripley's Believe It Or Not! Call Hallettsville the "13" city?

A. At one time, the city was all about the number 13. In 1913, it had 13 letters in its name. Its population was 1,300; it contained 13 saloons, 13 churches, and 13 newspapers. Lucky!

Q. What infamous woman was known as "The Bandit Queen" in the late 1800s and was notorious for her thieving ways (and was "The Hanging Judge" Isaac Parker's nemesis)?

A. Belle Starr, who was born Myra Belle Shirley.

POLITICS, TRANSPORTATION, AND MILITARY TALES

Before Brownsville Was Brownsville . . .

According to the official Texas Travel Guide, the Texas Historical Society named the city of Brownsville the second most important city in Texas history. This is because in March 28, 1846, General Zachary Taylor (who was to become the twelfth president of the United States) placed the U.S. flag on land that was then part of Matamoros, Mexico, claiming the Rio Grande as the official border between the two countries and that part of Matamoros as part of the United States. He built a fort on the site, later named Fort Brown after Major Jacob Brown. The town on the site later became known as Brownsville.

Taylor's action signaled the beginning of the Mexican-American War, which lasted until 1848. The American victory catapulted Taylor to the presidency in 1849, but there was one thing he could not conquer: death. That general claimed Taylor just 16 months after he took office.

Touring Brownsville today, you will see many historical buildings and museums that hark back to Taylor's time, when Brownsville was such a focal point of Texas history. Zachary Taylor Park is the place where Taylor and his troops made camp under live oak trees. The Historic Brownsville Museum has exhibits featuring many aspects of the Mexican-American War. Fort Brown itself still exists, even serving throughout the Civil War (both governments) and World War II. The fort's hospital building is now the administration building of Texas Southmost College, and several other buildings are part of the University of Texas at Brownsville.

Oh—and as far as Brownsville's relationship with Matamoros goes, both cities are on friendly terms and encourage tourism back and forth via several bridges connecting two cities, two countries, and two cultures.

Taming the West with an Apron String: Harvey Girls

Fred Harvey, a native of England, arrived in the United States at the age of 15 and began working first in the restaurant business and then in the railroad business. As he traveled by rail through the Southwest, he discovered the food to be mediocre and the service below par.

When he met with Charlie Morse, the president of the newly formed Atchison, Topeka, & Santa Fe Railway, Harvey proposed that he establish restaurants beside the tracks at stops along the way. The deal was settled with a handshake.

Harvey opened his restaurants throughout the Southwest—including Texas—and his waitresses weren't simply waitresses; they were culture wearing an apron. The Harvey Girls had to qualify for a position by showing good moral character, grace, charm, and other attributes that Fred Harvey thought important for women working with the traveling public.

The Harvey Girls became a Western icon, so much so that at least one movie has been made about them (the 1946 Harvey Girls, starring Judy Garland and Angela Lansbury), and there are books out the proverbial wazoo (including even a novel for young adults, written by Sheila Wood Foard, entitled Harvey Girl). The Harvey restaurant buildings in Texas still exist, but most are abandoned.

Some of them are under renovation and are being made into museums. One notable one is the Santa Fe Depot Museum in Gainesville.

For more on the Harvey Girls and how they helped, in the words of Fred Harvey, to "civilize the old West," see the "Virtual Texas section" at the back of this book.

The Blue Ghost

Everything, it seems, is bigger in Texas. In Corpus Christi Bay, the USS Lexington is no exception. The flight deck is so huge, you could conduct three football games on it simultaneously. The ship is 19 stories tall and is capable of carrying enough fuel to sail 30,000 miles before refueling. In World War II, Tokyo Rose called her the Blue Ghost. Commissioned in 1943, the Lexington has served longer than any other carrier in U.S. naval history (she was decommissioned in 1991) and has set more records than all others as well. This proud vessel was the first carrier to

The USS Lexington in her moorings. Courtesy Bryan Tumlinson.

enter Tokyo Bay, right after Japan signed the treaty with the United States in 1945—and when Tokyo Rose had been forever silenced by the free and the brave.

The vessel has other firsts too: It has sailed more miles than any other aircraft carrier in the world—209,000 miles. It was the first carrier to establish an oceangoing high school (in 1967) and to have women crew members onboard (in 1980).

Today, you can tour the Lexington, enjoy the thrill of a flight simulator (not for the faint of heart), eat in the ship's café, and even stay overnight because she's now a permanent resident of Corpus Christi.

The Unsung Heroes of Battle

When they think about large vessels that go into battle, most people consider the accoutrements of war: the turrets, the guns, the thickness of the hull, and speed capability. They also usually focus on those who fought.

There are other heros aboard battleships, though, who serve on another kind of front line: the cooks and galley staff members. Cooking three meals a day for several thousand hungry sailors is no small feat. Organizing and planning to have enough ingredients for all those meals, and for months at sea, would be a daunting task even for a general. For example, one recipe for pumpkin pie alone for a battleship's crew would require this kind of volume:

> *6 cases of canned pumpkin*
> *100 pounds of sugar*
> *30 gallons of water*
> *30 dozen eggs*
> *22 pounds of cornstarch*

My chef's hat is off to these unsung heroes.

DID YOU KNOW?

Both Sides of History

The site of the beginning of the Mexican-American War—the Palo Alto Battlefield National Historic Site—is the only unit of the National Park Service dedicated to tell the story of this conflict. You can find exhibits at the site telling the story of the conflict from both sides' perspectives.

A Peaceful Settlement of a Border Quandary

When the Mexican-American War ended, politicians drew a boundary from the Pacific Ocean to the west and to the Gulf of Mexico to the east. Part of this boundary included 1,000 miles of the Rio Grande. Both sides agreed: The deepest part of the river would be the line separating the two countries. Back then, the rule seemed very simple and easy to abide by.

Things grew muddled when Mother Nature, as she is wont to do, stepped in, and the river shifted its course many times over the years because of spring floods and erosion. Trying to accommodate this shift, politicians said that if the change happened over time, they would alter the boundary lines, but if the river changed course suddenly, as in the case of flooding, they would keep the place of the original deepest channel as the international boundary— even if it was no longer under water at all!

Over time, the Rio Grande and the boundaries were quite different, and land on both sides was increasingly in dispute as to which country owned it. The establishment of the International Boundary Commission in 1889 did little to help matters. In 1911, with tensions mounting, the border issue was brought before arbitration, but the resulting decision about where the border lay was disputed by the U.S. government. The matter remained a point of contention for 50 more years.

The area known as Chamizal was caught in the middle of a battle of morals and wills. In 1962, in recognition of the growing problem with Cuba, U.S. President John F. Kennedy decided to work to improve relations with Mexico and settle the issue once and for all.

In 1963 at the Chamizal Convention, Kennedy met with the president of Mexico, Adolfo López Mateos, to discuss the land that had been a point of contention for more than 100 years. They forged a treaty that relocated the Rio Grande back to its original channel and established its banks in a concrete-like bed. This led to a celebration of diversity that continues today.

In August 2007, President George W. Bush interrupted his Texas vacation to meet with Mexico President Felipe Calderón and Canada Prime Minister Stephen Harper with a purpose similar to the original Chamizal Convention: They brainstormed on cooperative ways to bolster the economy, increase border security, and other issues.

Now, in El Paso, the 55-acre Chamizal National Memorial commemorates the convention and treaty of 1963. There is a visitor center, all kinds of exhibits celebrating the divergence of cultures, and a permanent place for the Rio Grande international boundary. The Chamizal Festival, a celebration of this border region and its peoples, is held every October and includes dancing, music, and cultural demonstrations.

Now, visitors touring El Paso can easily visit Juárez, Mexico, on the same day by taking the El Paso–Juárez Trolley. Because of the peaceful settlement of the boundary issue, tourists can shop in El Paso in the morning and see a bullfight in Juárez in the afternoon.

Olé!

Border Crossing

The only legal border crossing between El Paso and Del Rio is at Presidio.

Before They Even Had Chads to Count!

It was the election of 1948, and the young Texas congressman with a reputation for ruthlessness was running for a seat in the U.S. Senate against the former governor of Texas, a man named Coke Stevenson. Election day, August 28, showed the young man defeated by more than 100 votes. On September 2, though, the Dallas Morning News headline read "Stevenson's Margin Firm," declaring him the clear winner.

But . . . there's more to the story. On September 3, it was announced that the votes from a small town west of Corpus Christi (Alice, current population approximately 19,000) hadn't been counted . . . or at least hadn't been counted completely, for Jim Wells County submitted an amended return.

From the ballot box (box 13) in Alice, the hopeful young politician received an additional 200 votes and Coke Stevenson received 2, and the man everyone thought had lost the election actually won, by a margin of 87 votes. Later, political humorists gave a name to this election gone awry: "the 87 votes that changed history."

Downright finagling? Author Robert Caro, who's writing an exhaustive series of history tomes dedicated to the life and political times of this man, thinks so. In his work, he points out that the election judge for precinct 13 was none other than Luis Salas, a member of the "good ol' boy network" and a friend to the ruthless politician. Years later—1986 to be exact—Caro interviewed Salas, who was 84 years old by then and admitted to stealing the votes. It was too late, by this time, to change history, for history had already been made and set in stone.

Who was the young politician? Lyndon Baines Johnson, who would go on to become the president of the United States.

The story was recounted by Contributing Editor Scott Sherman in the May/June 2002 issue of Columbia Journalism Review, who wrote about Caro and his life's work.

Sometimes it takes historians time to catch up with history.

Wrong Way Corrigan

The aviator who became famous for his attempt at flying solo—not as he planned, from New York to Long Beach California, but to Ireland—was from Galveston. Despite his huge mistake, once back in Galveston, the man history knows as "Wrong Way Corrigan" was given a parade.

By the way, his birth name was Clyde Groce Corrigan before he changed it to Douglas Corrigan.

Oh, to What Heights They Will Go: The Story of Rainbow Bridge

Bridge City used to be known as Prairie View before the overpass known as Rainbow Bridge was built. Completed in 1938, the bridge spans the Neches River and joins Texas's Port Arthur and Louisiana's Orange County.

When plans were being made to build the bridge, city officials must have been dismayed to discover a law that would change the design in the bridge. The law back then stated that any bridge built over a navigable body of water had to be able to accommodate the tallest ship in existence built by the U.S. Navy. At that time, the tallest ship was one used to moor dirigibles (known as a dirigible tender), so the bridge's clearance was set at 176 feet.

Rainbow Bridge is still the tallest bridge in Texas—and used to be the tallest in the country. The irony is this: That dirigible tender has yet to sail under the Rainbow Bridge, because it has never even been on the Neches River!

Your tax dollars at work.

Floating History

She's beautiful and big and has an equally large history. The she that I'm referring to is the Battleship Texas. Fashioned after HMS Dreadnought, she was commissioned just before World War I. World War II found her serving as flagship in the D-Day invasion of 1944, under the command of Denison native General Dwight D. Eisenhower, who as you know, later became President of the United States.

Now permanently moored at the San Jacinto Battleground State Historic Site, the Battleship Texas is a rare kind of monument: It is the last surviving pre–World War I dreadnought in the world. When you visit, give her a salute. She's earned it.

Ten-Hut!

During World War II, Gainesville was the location for Camp Howze, which was one of the largest infantry replacement training facilities in the country.

First Woman

The first female governor of Texas was Miriam A. "Ma" Ferguson. Her life and times are chronicled in the Bell County Museum, in Belton.

Haunting Oratory

When Ann Richards was speaking at the Democratic National Convention in 1988, she remarked of George H.W. Bush, "Poor George, he can't help it—he was born with a silver foot in his mouth." Two years later, she ran for governor of Texas and won.

Her remark, however, was destined to haunt her: In 1994, she found herself running for reelection. This time it was against George's son, George W. Bush. She lost the race.

Bridging the Centuries

For years, the only crossing possible at the Brazos River (in Waco) was a suspension bridge, built in 1870. Though today there are modern roads and bridges, the old bridge still exists, but as a pedestrian bridge. What used to help cowboys and cattle travel over the river is now part of a pleasurable stroll.

Governor for a Day; in the History Books Forever

On February 21, 1936, a baby girl was born to the Reverend Benjamin and Arlynne Jordan in Houston. Although poor, the child was raised with strict discipline and was taught that with hard work, she could achieve anything.

When she graduated from Phillis Wheatley High School, the young girl attended Texas Southern University, where she discovered that debating was one of her strong points. She and her teammates on the school debate team won awards at nearly every competition.

Graduating magna cum laude in 1956, the young student went on to study law at Boston University, and when she graduated from law school in 1959, the civil rights movement was nearing its apex. The law graduate decided that to effect change, she should enter politics, and she soon became friends with a vice-presidential candidate from Texas named Lyndon Baines Johnson.

After Johnson became vice-president under John F. Kennedy, the woman ran for a seat in the state Senate but was defeated in both 1962 and 1964. On her third attempt, she won; she was sworn in as the first black state senator since 1883.

The 37-year-old began to effect changes and improvements in people's living conditions and to protect everyone's civil rights—not just those of African Americans but also those of Native Americans, Hispanics, and other groups often overlooked and unprotected. Although she had many other achievements, such as becoming the first black woman from a southern state to serve in Congress and serving on the impeachment committee of President Richard M. Nixon, her greatest day was when she was sworn in as governor of Texas.

The young politician had been elected president pro tempore, or temporary president, of the Senate and, as such, was to be sworn in as governor only if the governor and lieutenant governor were both out of state. This happened on June 10, 1972.

Now you know that although she was one of the greatest leaders to come out of Texas in the tumultuous civil rights era, the woman we remember as Barbara Charline Jordan also was governor of Texas . . . for a day.

Supporting Soldiers' Families at Fort Sam Houston

San Antonio's Brooke Army Medical Center is located at Fort Sam Houston. In 2007, Brooke made medical and military history when it broke ground for its one-of-a-kind Warrior and Family Support Center.

Brooke is the U.S. Army's only burn unit and has an

amputee center as well, but never before has there been a center for families—parents, wives, children of soldiers—to stay while their loved ones receive treatment for their injuries sustained while in the line of duty.

The 12,000-square-foot unit has received the support of U.S. Representative Charles A. Gonzalez, who participated in the September 2007 groundbreaking. The commander of Fort Sam Houston told Associate Press reporters that this would be a place for families and soldiers to heal and rebuild their lives, torn apart by war, a place where loved ones could stay and be close to their returning heroes while they mended.

Taking the Scenic Route

The first officially designated scenic highway in Texas is State Highway 4, which runs north and south through the center of Palo Pinto County. Travelers along this route enjoy the views of rolling hills, blazing foliage colors in the fall and flamboyant wildflowers in the spring.

Texas—Unique Among the States!

Texas is the only state to have entered the Union by treaty instead of the "usual" way, by territorial annexation.

Hanging' at the Hangar

The town of Big Spring was the site once known as Hangar 25. Between 1942 and 1945, Hangar 25 was part of the Big Spring Army Air Corps Bombardier School, which trained more than 6,000 cadets. It's now a museum with rotating exhibits throughout the year.

The Paul Revere of Texas

Juan Seguin is known as the Paul Revere of Texas because Sam Houston sent him to warn settlers that Antonio Lopez de Santa Anna was coming. The town of Seguin honored him by naming the town after him, and there is a bronze sculpture there in his honor. You can also see where he is buried, on the hill near the coliseum.

Dallas, the Assassination, and a Generation's Lost Innocence

November 22, 1963, has been referred to as the 9/11 (the terrorist attacks of September 11, 2001) of two generations ago. I remember hearing of President Kennedy's being shot and our teacher at Bellaire Elementary School in San Antonio bursting into tears during the telling. Later, being out of school to honor the fallen president, I and millions of other schoolchildren (along with their parents) watched live as alleged killer Lee Harvey Oswald was escorted by marshals and saw Jack Ruby shoot him point-blank and kill him, also live.

Dallas has long sought to change its image, to not be seen only as the city where a beloved president was assassinated. Although the assassination could have happened anywhere—historians say that Kennedy refused to ride in any kind of armored vehicle when taking part in a parade—for decades, many people associated this fine city only with the place where Kennedy was assassinated.

The city and its citizens have a new image in the twenty-first century, but the myriad of conspiracy theories still persist and will probably never fade. Even as recently as May 2007, Reuters reporter David Morgan wrote an article about some researchers reconsidering the hard evidence in the case that, according to the Warren Commission, claimed that Oswald acted alone and that there were no other assassins, on the grassy knoll or elsewhere. Their conclusion was just like the conclusions of other investigations before them: "Evidence used to rule out a second assassin is . . . flawed."

Did Oswald act alone? Was he the fall guy, and did Ruby kill him to silence him? Who were the others—if there were others? If there is anything that haunts Dallas citizens, historians, or American citizens who witnessed that part of history, it is this unsettled question—which will probably always remain so.

When you visit Dallas, maybe you can find some answers for yourself, in the exhibits relating to this tragedy at the Sixth Floor Museum located at the former Texas School Book Depository.

George W. Bush Lived Here . . . and Here

The cities of Midland and Odessa can both lay claim to fame as places where George W. lived before becoming a U.S. president. In 1947, George H.W. Bush and his wife Barbara brought their family to live in Odessa; they later moved to Midland. Later, son George W. Bush and his wife Laura lived in Midland, a city to which they retain emotional ties—according to the tour guide anyway.

Strange But True!

The Infamous Archives War

In the days of early Texas, one of the decisions the people were obliged to make was the site for their permanent capital. The Texas Congress wanted a place in the state's center, but Republican President Sam Houston's idea was to place it in—where else?— his namesake city, Houston.

In 1839, after Mirabeau B. Lamar became the

next president of the republic, though, he sided with Congress. That same year, five scouts were sent to do a reconnaissance of central Texas, and the site was chosen to place the capital near Waterloo, which later became Austin. (See "The 'Waterloo' of Texas" in Chapter 2 for more on Waterloo.) In a few months, Congress had moved there, holding meetings in rustic log cabins. In September of that year, the archives and furnishings for the permanent capital were moved from Houston to Austin, using 50 ox-drawn carts.

None of this would seem important to anyone who did not take into account that a county seat, capital, or town hall site is nothing without its archives—its official historical documents. A war over these documents ensued, escalating over the years to the point of violence.

In 1841, Sam Houston again became president, but he refused to move to the official residence in Austin: In protest of Austin's being the capital, he instead took rooms at a local boardinghouse under the management of Mrs. Angelina Eberly (Houston would soon come to regret this decision, as you will see).

He referred to Austin as, in the words of the Texas State Library and Archives Commission, "the most unfortunate site on earth for a seat of government," and apparently many other Texans agreed with him. Houston and those of his ilk had only to wait for an opportune moment to seize the archives and take them to Houston, making that city the official capital.

They did not have long to wait: In 1841, the Mexican army invaded, taking control of San Antonio and two other cities, Goliad and Victoria. Sam Houston spoke before a special session of Congress, saying that the city of Houston stood a better chance than Austin of being defended against the southern invaders by virtue of geography, and he ordered the secretary of state to bring the archives to Houston.

On learning of this plan, the citizens of Austin formed a committee of their own—a vigilante committee they called the Committee of Safety. They stood poised to deter any attempt to remove the archives from Austin and warned everyone that any such attempts would be met with violent resistance.

In December 1842, Houston's group, led by Captain Eli Chandler and Colonel Thomas I. Smith, traveled to Austin with 20 men. Their mission: get all the archives loaded onto wagons and bring them to Houston.

Chandler and Smith and their men had three of the wagons loaded without incident when Mrs. Eberly spotted them and fired a cannon, thereby sending a signal to the Committee of Safety. The committee members chased Houston's men and their wagons; the men surrendered at gunpoint just outside Austin. The committee members then took the archives and returned them to Austin. Records say that the citizens then celebrated their victory with a New Year's Eve party.

There's more to the story, though: The incident was investigated by a select committee of the Texas House of Representatives in January 1843, and the result was a document "highly critical" of the conduct of Sam Houston and his men, but the full House rejected this report and its findings by a vote of 19–18. The issue of placement of a permanent capital was not firmly (or legally) decided until 1850, when the citizens of the state of Texas voted to make Austin their capital city.

Angelina Eberly fires the cannon during the infamous "Archives War." Courtesy Texas State Library and Archives Commission. Artist: D. W. C. Baker, 1875.

. . . And More on This Subject

The town of Henrietta, in the Panhandle Plains area of Texas, had its own archives war. In 1873, the town of Henrietta was reorganized, having relocated to an area relatively safer from Indian attacks. The people of Cambridge disagreed with Henrietta's being set up as the county seat, so they stole the courthouse records. Legend says that a group of cowboys hightailed it from Henrietta to Cambridge, roped the safe holding the records, and dragged it back to Henrietta.

Two "Rights" and a Wrong Choice

During the presidential election year of 1844, Henry Clay traveled through the South, campaigning. He was very popular, and thousands came to hear him speak. At the time, Texas was being considered for statehood, which Clay vehemently opposed.

As the time approached for the decision to be made about Texas's statehood, Clay wrote a letter that was to be printed in whatever newspaper would run it. His letter warned legislators that if the United States admitted Texas into the Union, the country would end up at war with Mexico. His advisors told him not to send the letter to the media, saying this would cost him the presidency. He is said to have retorted, "I would rather be right than president!" and mailed the letter nonetheless.

He and his advisors were both right. The United States annexed Texas in 1845, went to war with Mexico the following year, and Clay lost the presidential race to James K. Polk, a North Carolinian.

Texans must have thought a lot of his stance and the fact that he had the courage of his convictions, for Clay County, Texas, is named after him. If you get to the county seat of Henrietta and stroll the grounds surrounding the beautiful courthouse, perhaps you'll want to send a mental salute to Henry Clay, who stood by his beliefs despite the consequences.

The Legend of the Noninaugural Speech

As you have probably surmised from reading the stories of the clashes between Mirabeau B. Lamar and Sam Houston (see "The Infamous Archives War" story earlier in this chapter), they weren't exactly best friends. Sometimes they went to great lengths just to show how they felt about each other. What happened at the inauguration of Lamar, who was replacing Sam Houston as president of the Republic of Texas in 1838, was one notable example of this.

Houston had apparently decided early on that he would not only attend the inauguration but also, as the saying goes, steal the show. He dressed in an elaborate green-and-gold outfit, complete with matching cap, which by itself would have been sufficiently ostentatious.

He went a step further, however. The story goes that Houston gave a speech that went on so long (several hours, the accounts say) that the new president was unable, because of time constraints, to give his own inaugural address.

Incidentally, the outfit Houston wore is currently on display at the Sam Houston Museum in Huntsville.

Where It All Started: Old Washington

The town formerly known as Old Washington or Washington-on-the-Brazos and now simply called Washington (population approximately 270) was where the Texas Declaration of Independence was signed, and where the first constitution for the new republic was drafted. The draft was written by George Campbell Childress in a blacksmith shop owned by Noah T. Byars. Washington-on-the-Brazos was also the capital of the republic from 1842 to 1846.

You can visit the place where all this history was made and see its museum (Star of the Republic Museum), park (Washington-on-the-Brazos State Historic Site), and a living history farm (on the park site). For such a small town, it's bursting with interesting historical things to see related to Texas.

And precisely because the town is so small, you're sure to get a big Texas welcome.

The Birthplace of the Texas Flag

This title is claimed by Montgomery, Texas. The flag was designed by Montgomery resident Dr. Charles Bellinger Stewart, who also designed the official state seal. Dr. Stewart also had the honor of being the first to sign Texas's Declaration of Independence.

At the Nathan H. Davis Pioneer Complex and Museum, you can see a copy of Stewart's original drawing of the flag.

This Is Not a Ferry Tale!

Before technology developed bridges to make crossing rivers easy, there were ferries. Some you boarded, and
they steamed to the other side. Before that, though, there
were "hand-pulled" ferries. There is only one of them still
in existence in the Western hemisphere.

In the town of Los Ebanos, near Brownsville, there is
a toll bridge, but there you will find this unusual ferry. The
ferry will hold up to three cars, and for $1.50 you can share
the experience your grandparents and great-grandparents
had: watch the crew pull the ferry, hand-over-hand, across
the river by a rope that goes from one bank to the other.

If you're looking for an unusual way to arrive in
Mexico from Texas (or vice versa), the Los Ebanos ferry
is it!

The "Waterloo" of Texas

After the state became the Republic of Texas, it began to boom, attracting settlers from all over the country
and the world. One city in particular, Waterloo, attracted
one Mirabeau B. Lamar from Georgia to come settle in the
new republic, having been invited to come stay by friend
James Fannin after Lamar, a state senator, had lost his
wife to tuberculosis.

Before he left Georgia to move to Texas, though,
Lamar heard the terrible news about the massacre at the
Alamo (see "Remember the Alamo!" in Chapter 3 for that
story). Legendary figures such as Davy Crockett and James
Bowie were killed, and Lamar's friend Fannin, along with
his soldiers from Fort Goliad, were tracked down and ambushed by Antonio Lopez de Santa Anna and his men.

Lamar immediately joined the Texas Army in time
for the Battle of San Jacinto, in which Texas emerged victorious, and Lamar began making a name for himself. Ris-

ing from private to colonel in the Texas Army, Lamar was made secretary of war in the cabinet, then vice-president of Texas under Sam Houston. Running for president after Houston's second term in office, Lamar became president of the Republic of Texas in 1838—after the other two candidates committed suicide before election day. One candidate, James Collinsworth, drowned in Galveston Bay in what is generally thought to have been a suicide attempt. Two days before Collinsworth's death, second opposing candidate Peter Grayson took his own life while in Bean Station, Tennessee.

Lamar's burning ambitions were twofold: First, he wanted the city of Waterloo to be the new capital of the Republic and named in honor of Stephen F. Austin; second, he wanted to further education in Texas.

The man history books call a Renaissance man got his way; the town was renamed Austin and then was voted the permanent capital in 1872. Lamar himself became known as the "Father of Texas Education," a title that became official in 1881 when Austin was chosen as the site for the University of Texas, now the largest public university in the state.

Hangin' It Up in Fredericksburg

If you want to travel back in time—say, to the World War II era—you might want to spend some time in Gillespie County's Hangar Hotel. The hotel has been designed to look like a World War II-era hangar for airplanes, and was built to resemble an old wooden hangar at Brooks Air Force Base in San Antonio.

Guests at the Hangar Hotel get the full World War II experience—on approaching the grounds, they see the South Pacific–style landscaping, complete with palm trees, sleep in beds made up with the old olive-green army blankets, and use rotary-dial telephones. The hotel's diner is also in keeping with the time period; diners have a view of the water tower, searchlight, and runway. There are vintage planes galore too: Even the front of the hotel is graced with a 1946 Navion.

This kind of hotel is for people who want an experience—not just a place to stay the night.

In the Name of Temperance

In the city of San Antonio, there's a bar inside the Menger Hotel that is designed to look exactly like London's House of Lords Pub, but that's not what it is best known for: In her antidrinking crusade, temperance advocate Carrie Nation took an axe to the bar there one night. You can still see the axe mark in the cherrywood.

The Haunted Governor's Mansion

Built in 1856, the governor's mansion, located at 1010 Colorado Street in Austin, was constructed in beautiful, classic Greek Revival style, with ornate columns gracing the entryway and a large verandah. Among its claims to fame are that it is the oldest remaining public building in the downtown area and the fourth-oldest governor's residence in continuous occupation in the country.

It has something else too that most people don't know about: One of the former governors—Sam Houston, to be exact—is said to continue to occupy the residence. He's not the only spirit said to wander the halls either: Former Governor Pendleton Murrah, who was governor from 1863 to 1865, had a nephew who, crushed after rejection by a young woman he'd hoped to marry, committed suicide in one of the bedrooms upstairs.

The mansion is open for tours from 10:00 am to noon, Monday through Thursday. When you visit the mansion, keep your eyes open!

Before Kitty Hawk, There Was Luckenbach

Decades before the Wright brothers' historic flight on the coast of North Carolina, an immigrant with a curious, inventive mind arrived in Texas. Born in Württemberg, Germany, in 1821, Jacob Frederick Brodbeck immigrated to Texas in 1846, settling in Gillespie County, where he was a schoolteacher.

After marrying a former student and having 12 children with her, Brodbeck went on to become a variety of things, including county commissioner, county surveyor, and district school supervisor. He was fascinated with the idea that human flight was possible, and this consumed every spare minute of his time.

In 1863, Brodbeck perfected a small model plane he referred to as an airship, complete with a coil-spring-operated propeller, wings, and a rudder. That same year the Brodbecks moved to San Antonio, where the young inventor displayed his airship at local fairs, delighting his audiences. Encouraged by the public's interest, Brodbeck gained financial backing from three local men to enable him to construct a full-size airship, one that would carry a person. They, of course, hoped to profit when his invention became successful, at which time he could patent his airship.

The full-size airship was completed in 1865, and what happened after that is subject to debate and speculation, for there are basically three different accounts of Brodbeck's attempted first flight. The first account claims that when Brodbeck's airship went airborne in a field about three miles east of Luckenbach, it rose 12 feet in the air and flew for approximately 100 feet before the airship crashed. The second account says that Brodbeck's first flight happened in San Antonio in San Pedro Park but that as in the first account the craft crashed. To complicate matters a bit further, the third account claims that the first flight occurred in 1868 rather than in 1865.

At any rate, Brodbeck's crashed airship was beyond repair. Try though he might, he could get no further financial backing from his three initial investors, and his subsequent efforts to obtain more investors were in vain. He went on a tour around the country to try to find other investors, but his diagrams and papers with details were stolen while he was in Michigan.

Brodbeck returned to his land in Luckenbach, where he learned of the Wright brothers' successful flight in 1903. Brodbeck passed away in 1910 and was buried on his farm.

Although little artifacts remain of what the would-be aviator accomplished with his airship design, there is a monument to his achievement in the form of a bust of Brodbeck in San Pedro Park and another in his adopted home town of Fredericksburg.

If he had had better luck, a professional publicist, and more money, Brodbeck would have put Texas in the first chapter of aviation's history book.

. . . And One More Aviator's Story

The people of Pittsburg, Texas, have embraced one of their own as another of aviation's pioneers: the Reverend Burrell Cannon. Like many people of the era—which held out promises of huge monetary rewards and fame for constructing an aircraft that could carry people—he was also fascinated with the possibility of flight.

Cannon's aircraft was inspired in part by a quote from Ezekiel 1:19 of the Bible (King James Version), which reads, "And when the living creatures went, the wheels went by them: and when the living creatures were lifted up from the earth, the wheels were lifted up." This was a partial description of a vision that the prophet Ezekiel experienced, and the scripture fired the imagination of the young minister, who also had a flair for anything having to do with engineering.

Cannon finished his prototype of an aircraft in 1902, a year before the Wright brothers' flight. It had a four-cylinder gas engine that drove paddles to turn wheels, and sails for wings. Legend has it that Cannon was away, giving a sermon, when foundry employees took the plane for its initial spin into the air. Some accounts say the plane flew about 160 feet at a height of approximately 12 feet, before vibrations became so violent that the pilot turned off the engine and floated the plane to the ground. Fearing the loss of their jobs, all witnesses and participants are said to have taken a vow of silence about the flight.

Cannon was in the midst of sending his airship around the country (one of its stops being the St. Louis World's Fair), garnering funds for his invention, when a storm in Texarkana chewed the airship from its perch on a rail car. Although Cannon made a second attempt with a new airship in 1913, he eventually abandoned his dream.

The Pittsburg Optimist Club constructed a replica of the original airship for the 1986 Texas Sesquicentennial; when you go to Pittsburg, you can see the replica on display in the Northeast Texas Rural Heritage Center and Museum.

Imagination Took Flight Here

It was just after World War II, and some young men who had been pilots during the war came back to the Odessa area as crop dusters. In 1957, a few of them, longing for the good ol' days, collected their money and bought an old airplane—a P-51D Mustang. They came up with an idea: get together the most complete collection of World

War II–era combat planes ever in one place.

The idea sounded simple enough, until the group discovered that almost all the combat aircraft used in the war effort—nearly 300,000—had been destroyed. They resolved to find, renovate, and exhibit at least one model of every aircraft used in World War II for future generations to learn about and be inspired by.

That incredible project has resulted in the American Airpower Heritage Museum and Commemorative Air Force (CAF) headquarters, located at the Midland International Airport. The CAF has at least 140 different aircraft, displaying them on a rotating basis, and an impressive array of aircraft-nose art. The CAF holds an annual air show every October as well.

Because of a handful of dedicated, visionary World War II pilots, the United States has a supreme aviation museum, and every day the seed is planted in young minds for their owners to take to the air themselves.

In the Middle of Things

If you want to be in the middle of things, then you want to live in Brady, for it's about as close to the center of the state as you can get. Just to make sure you know exactly where it is, the Texas Society of Professional Surveyors surveyed the state, then placed a marker designating the geographic center of Texas in the town.

The Heart of Texas Museum carries the town's nickname, along with all kinds of exhibits relating to the town's and the state's early days.

The Capitol Building: Don't Take It for Granite.

According to the State Preservation Board in Austin, the building that is the epitome of the law and administration of the Lone Star State was completed in 1888.

The beautiful granite (called Texas pink) was hauled to the construction site by rail from 50 miles away (mined at Marble Falls's Granite Mountain). The Renaissance Revival structure has a limestone base, and the building is such an impressive sight that it is against the law to build anything that would obstruct the view from just about anywhere in the city.

This pink granite building is the Capitol Building. Courtesy of the State Preservation Board.

Like everything else in Texas, the Capitol Building is big. In terms of square footage, it is larger than any other state capital in the nation. But the most fascinating fact about the Capitol Building to me is this: The dome is higher than any other capitol dome in the nation, including the one in the District of Columbia (it's 14 feet taller than Washington's dome)! When I asked Governor Richard Perry's office about this, his office workers only smiled—a big Texas smile.

Harlingen, Where War and Art Come Together

The amazing life of Felix de Weldon, born in Vienna, Austria, is probably known only in art circles. Recognized as a genius in art at the age of six, he was sent to study the masters, and he went on to travel the world while continuing his studies. His work is unique in that it was displayed at Buckingham Palace while the artist still lived.

He became a U.S. citizen in 1945 and entered the U.S. Navy, serving as a naval aviation artist. It was in Maryland that he came across a Pulitzer prize–winning picture taken by news photographer Joseph Rosenthal of the soldiers raising the American flag at Iwo Jima. De Weldon was inspired and initially created a three-foot tall, three-dimensional model of the event.

He created another model, nine feet tall, in plaster; this model toured the country. When Congress realized the genius behind this work, it commissioned de Weldon to create a 48-foot-tall monument. It took him nine years to complete it and became the masterpiece of his life.

The Flag Raising on Iwo Jima now stands in Arlington, Virginia, as the Marine Corps War Memorial, but Texas has a jewel of its own in relation to this masterpiece.

In Harlingen, site of the Marine Military Academy, the Iwo Jima Memorial and Museum is home to the original model of this famous statue, and it was donated to the academy by the sculptor himself. Although the sculptor passed away in 2003, you can visit his statue, see a video about the battle victory, and tour the museum, where art and military history converge.

(Still) Lighting the Way . . .

In 1895, Austin lit its streets with 31 carbon-arc lamps. Tall enough to give light up to a radius of 3,000 feet, the so-called moonlight towers were 165 feet tall. Today, the lights use mercury vapor instead of carbon, and although only 17 of them are still intact, Austin is now the only city in the country that continues to use moonlight towers for light.

Your Perfect Answer to "Are We There Yet?"

Adrian is the city at the midpoint of the famous

Route 66. As you're driving through Adrian and the kids ask "Are we there yet?" you can answer, "Well, we're halfway there," and you'll be all the way right.

Eden, Home to (at Least Two) Heroes

Eden, Texas, in the Panhandle Plains area, is home to at least two military heroes: James Earl Rudder, who led the U.S. Army Rangers to scale the cliffs of Normandy, silencing German gunners during the D-Day invasion of World War II, and Ira Eaker, who was the pioneer in creating technology for planes to refuel in-flight.

Both were generals—what do you expect?—and a marker in town honors these two noble patriots. Rudder was also the mayor of Brady from 1946 to 1952 and the sixteenth president of Texas A&M University, serving from 1959 through 1970.

Wiley Post: Aviation Hero

Born in Van Zandt County, Texas, Wiley Post began parachuting for a flying circus, Burrell Tibbs and his Texas Topnotch Fliers. Post met Will Rogers in a rodeo; they became close friends.

Post flew around the world in 1931, making record time, and wrote a book about it entitled <u>Around the World in Eight Days</u>, for which Will Rogers wrote the introduction. He later piloted a plane that crashed in Alaska, killing himself and passenger Will Rogers.

A historical marker in Grand Saline details Post's life and accomplishments.

Audie Murphy: World War II's Most Decorated Hero

Audie Leon Murphy, born in 1924, rose from humble roots as a son of a Texas sharecropper to become the most decorated hero of World War II. He was given at least 33 awards and decorations not only by the U.S. government but also by France and Belgium.

After his illustrious military career, he turned to acting and writing. His 1949 autobiography, entitled <u>To Hell and Back</u>, became a best seller. Tragically, he was killed in a plane crash in 1971 near Roanoke, Virginia.

In Greenville (near his birthplace), the Audie Murphy/American Cotton Museum contains many artifacts of his life, along with a 10-foot-tall statue of Murphy.

Q & A

Q. What military museum offers exhibits of all military branches and includes highlights from the Revolutionary War to the current day?

A. Freedom Museum USA, in Pampa

Q. What town is often called the Lexington of Texas, and why?

A. Gonzales, because it was the site of the first skirmish of the Texas Revolution

Q. What is the local name for the scenic drive that is Farm Road 170, stretches from Lajitas (in Big Bend Country) through Presidio, and is referred to by the state department of tourism as "one of the most spectacular drives in Texas"?

A. El Camino del Rio, which translates to "the River Road"

Q. What city is host to the only NATO pilot training program in the world?

A. Wichita Falls

Q. What city still refers to itself as "pearl of the prairie," a nickname from the days when Mexican cowboys would bring cattle to the area to be picked up at the railhead?

A. El Campo, which means "the Camp" in Spanish. It's still a center for agriculture, fishing, birding, and sightseeing (the town has more than 20 murals painted on the sides of its buildings).

Q. Where is the Center for Transportation and Commerce (Railroad Museum), complete with 35 vintage railcars, located?

A. In Galveston, in the area known as the Strand

Q. What is the name of the bridge that connects South Padre Island, Texas, to the mainland?

A. Queen Isabella Causeway—it's also the longest bridge in the state

Q. In what two cities in Texas can you tour the area by duck?

A. Galveston Island Duck Tours allows visitors to tour the area by a vehicle (named a Duck) that travels equally well on land and on water. Also, Austin Duck Adventures will take you to see the state capitol and the University of Texas at Austin, and then splash into Lake Austin for a tour of the shoreline!

Q. What was the nickname of the World War II–era aerial gunnery training program at Harlingen and Laredo?

A. Operation Pinball. The concept was to train aerial gunners by letting them actually shoot at real planes in mock combat.

Q. What museum in Lubbock is dedicated to the World War II military glider program?

A. Silent Wings Museum

Q. What hero of World War II, the commander in chief of the Pacific Fleet, was born in Fredericksburg?

A. Fleet Admiral Chester W. Nimitz

Q. What was the nickname for the San Benito & Rio Grande Valley Railway, given because of its intricate network of rail lines?

A. Spiderweb Railroad

Q. Where in Texas is one of the last remaining wooden railroad stations in the nation?

A. At the Santa Fe Museum in Santa Fe.

Q. What city is the starting point for the so-called Presidential Corridor, a highway, and why is this road given the name?

A. Austin is the starting place for U.S. Highway 290, Texas State Highway 21, which takes travelers to Bryan and College Station. The road connects the Lyndon Baines Johnson Library and Museum in Austin to the George Bush Presidential Library and Museum in College Station.

Q. What is the name of the drive along a ridge on U.S. Route 281 (officially, R.M. 32) in the Texas Hill Country?

A. The Devil's Backbone. It's one of the most scenic and dramatic drives in Texas.

Q. Who was the last president of the Republic of Texas?

A. Dr. Anson Jones. The town of Anson (in the Panhandle Plains) is named for him.

Q. What highway, now known as Old San Antonio Road, used to be called King's Highway (hint: it runs through Nacogdoches)?

A. El Camino Real, which was blazed by the first provincial

governor of Texas (Domingo Terán de los Ríos) in 1691

Q. What city holds the largest Veterans Day memorial service in the United States?

A. The city of Flatonia, in the Prairies and Lakes region.

Q. Who was the first African American to become a licensed pilot in not only the United States but also in the entire world?

A. Bessie Coleman, who grew up in Waxahachie, Texas

Q. Where in Texas was the site of the first mass parachute drop in history?

A. Brooks Air Force Base, San Antonio

BEFORE "THE" WAR

The Story of Cynthia Ann Parker . . .

It was at Parker's Fort, Texas, in 1836, that a handful of settlers were attacked by a raiding band of Comanche warriors, led by their chief, Peta Nocona. Although many of the settlers were killed, several were captured, among them a little girl.

Her name was Cynthia Ann Parker, and as is typical in captive psychology, the little girl quickly began to learn the ways of her captors, the Comanche people. Finally she was accepted by Comanches as one of their own. She adopted the name Naduah, and after she grew up, married Peta Nocona. They had three children, Quanah (meaning "fragrant"), Pecos (meaning "peanut"), and Topsannah (meaning "prairie flower"), and for some years, life was good.

Cynthia's life was once again turned upside down when soldiers found her and her people at their camp in Palo Duro Canyon in 1860. Although white people—usually trappers and hunters—had met her on several occasions before this and offered to negotiate her release, she had always refused to leave the life she had come to love. When soldiers discovered her and her people at the Pease River, after looking into Cynthia Ann's blue eyes, they realized this was the woman who had become a legend among white settlers. She was captured and taken to live with some of her former relatives. Peta Nocona, Quanah, and most of the men were away on a buffalo hunt and did not learn of Cynthia's Ann's being taken until their return to camp.

Topsannah died in 1861, within a year after being captured by the soldiers, and the grieving Cynthia Ann never recovered from the loss of her children and the loss of the free life she had known. Her relatives never allowed her to see her husband or sons again. In Anderson County, Texas, three years after Topsannah had "walked the spirit road," Cynthia Ann also died—some say of a broken heart. She was buried in Oklahoma, at Fort Sill, next to her little daughter, Topsannah.

. . . and of Quanah Parker

The young son of Cynthia Ann Parker and Comanche Chief Peta Nocona grew up in the free ways of the Comanche people. He learned how to ride a horse as soon as he could walk, and soon after, he learned the ways of the hunt and techniques in fighting and in war-making.

In 1861, Peta Nocona was mortally wounded in a raid against encroaching Apaches. Before he died, it is said that he told Quanah of his mixed ancestry and advised him to never trust the white settlers or the U.S. government. After Peta Nocona's death, his son Pecos went to live with one band, and Quanah, with another. After about a year, Quanah finally settled with the Comanche band known as the Quahadi, whose chief was Yellow Bear.

Yellow Bear had a beautiful daughter named was Wackeah, and Quanah loved her but could not pay the bride-price of 10 horses to Yellow Bear. When the young couple learned that Yellow Bear planned on giving Wackeah to another warrior who could pay the price, they eloped—taking with them nearly two dozen warriors, with the plan to make their own band. The two bands met in the spring of 1867 and instead of fighting to the death, decided to make peace and join forces against the white man. Quanah and his wife, along with the rebellious warriors, were once again part of the Quahadi band, and together they raided settlements and took livestock, earning the name "Red Raiders" among terrified white settlers.

Quanah Parker. Courtesy Arizona Historical Society.

The settlers appealed to the government for assistance in stemming the unending tide of raids against them and their property, and help was not long in forthcoming. In 1867, the U.S. government's newly formed Indian Peace Commission gathered with the five major tribes in the area—the Comanche among them—and signed the Treaty of Medicine Lodge, which basically confined the native peoples to reservations and farming for a living, instead of living wild and free, and guaranteed that the native people would give no further resistance to soldiers and settlers. Many of those in attendance did not want to sign such a document but were told by the white representatives—General William Tecumseh Sherman among them—that to attempt to stop white settlers' further encroachment would be about as useful as trying to stop the sun or the moon in their paths. (Although Quanah attended the treaty gathering, he did not sign the treaty or make a speech; he and others did not agree with the pact.) It was here that Quanah learned of his mother's death in 1864, whereupon he adopted his mother's surname.

Because Quanah's band was not represented by the treaty gathering, he and his band continued in their resistance. He and others went on the warpath, and the back-and-forth retaliation between his band and white soldiers became a bloody chess game. A turning point came when Quanah was gravely wounded during an attack on white buffalo hunters at Adobe Walls in 1874. It was in 1875 that, seeing the futility of further resistance, Quanah and his people surrendered at Fort Sill (now part of Oklahoma).

Quanah Parker went on to became one of the most celebrated Native Americans of his or any other time.

Quanah clung to his Indian roots while embracing aspects of "the white road" as well: He often dressed in modern business attire, he invested in a railroad, he hunted with President Theodore Roosevelt, and he became wealthy as he negotiated grazing rights with cattlemen. On his reservation, he became a judge settling disputes. Because of a vision he had after sustaining a grave wound during the Adobe Walls battle, he also founded the Native American Church (which involves a ritual using peyote), married four more wives, and had 25 children.

The last Comanche chief passed on to live with the Great Spirit in 1911 and is buried next to his mother. The inscription on his tombstone reads:

> *Resting here until day breaks*
> *And shadows fall and darkness*
> *Disappears is*

Quanah Parker, Last Chief
of the Comanches
Born 1852
Died February 23, 1911

There is much, however, that lives on in Quanah's remembrance. The town of Quanah, Texas, is named for the chief (and the city has the Quanah Parker Monument); the town of Nocona was named for his father, Chief Peta Nocona. Finally, because Quanah Parker had so many children, the Parker family reunions are renowned in the state—on both the Indian and the "white" sides.

DID YOU KNOW?

Meet Famous Folks

You can visit Cynthia Ann Parker—or at least a likeness of her—and other famous and infamous people important to Texas history at an experiential museum called Frontier Texas! in Abilene. The Spirit Gallery, one of the exhibits, lets you see and hear Parker, Doc Holliday, and others as they explore their part of history in the Lone Star State.

Guess What?

What fort, established in 1854 in Big Bend Country as the first military post to guard the way for those traveling between San Antonio and El Paso, is now a National Historic Site operated under auspices of the National Park Service?

It's Fort Davis National Historic Site. Deactivated in 1891, it remains one of the best examples of nineteenth-century frontier forts and is open for tours.

The Place Where Texas History Began . . .

The coast of southeast Texas is alive with birds and other wildlife, and the waters teem with fish ready for the taking. These factors, combined with a tropical climate and fertile soil, made this area the most desirable place for early Texans to make their home.

The first 300 Texas settlers, led by Stephen F. Austin, came ashore from their schooner, Lively, and made their home here near the Brazos River in 1821. This tenacious group of people forged a home out of wilderness and fought to make Texas a republic independent of Mexico. The area now known as West Columbia became the first capital of the Texas Republic (from September to December 1836) and is still a place popular for tourists, explorers, and people who want to make a life and not just a living. The original settlers will live forever in the annals of Texas history as the "Old Three Hundred."

The area today is known as Brazosport and consists of nine small towns: Freeport, West Columbia, Jones Creek, Surfside Beach, Lake Jackson, Richwood, Oyster Creek, Clute, and Quintana Beach.

Today, you can go visit the area where the Republic of Texas was born and learn more about it at places such as Columbia Historical Museum in West Columbia. Richmond, northwest of the Brazosport area, is the county seat; in Morton Cemetery there are the graves of many of the first settlers of Texas. One of them is Jane Herbert Wilkinson Long (1798–1880), known as the "Mother of Texas" because of the birth of her child in 1821 on the Bolivar Peninsula; her land grant covered most of what is Richmond today.

... Then There's "The Birthplace of Texas"

Deer Park claims to be the birthplace of Texas. Simon West founded Deer Park in 1892, naming it for the many deer to be found in the area, but the town calls itself the birthplace of Texas because the peace treaty between Texas and Mexico was drawn up here after the Battle of San Jacinto. A replica of the building where this happened has been erected in town. Called Patrick Cabin, it can be toured Monday through Friday. It's now located between 1302 Center Street and W. Helgra Street and was rededicated in April 2008.

... Then There's "The Cradle of Texas"

The town of San Augustine claims to be the cradle of Texas, and with good reason: The first governor of Texas (James P. Henderson) lived here, Sam Houston once had an office here, Davy Crockett was honored here while en route to the battle at the Alamo, and part of El Camino Real, the "King's Highway," runs through it.

Incidentally, Columbus also claims this title. Stephen F. Austin's "Old Three Hundred" colonists settled in this area too in the early 1820s.

That Famous Phrase

The phrase "Remember the Alamo!" was initially yelled by General Sidney Sherman, who was a cavalry officer. The town of Sherman is named in his honor.

(Quite Possibly) The Oldest Texas Man

Texans have proof that there were humans in their region as far back as 22,000 years ago. Anthropologist Fred Wendorf authenticated the remains of an ancient human whom people refer to as Midland Man, discovered on the property of Scharbauer Ranch south of the town of

Midland.

Midland Man—or at least what has been found of him—is on display at the Midland County Historical Museum.

. . . And the Oldest Texas Woman

Workers for the Texas Department of Transportation were digging to expand a road connecting Cedar Park to Round Rock and uncovered the ancient remains of a woman. Archeologists began working at the site and discovered more than 150 fireplaces and other evidence that this was a human residence long ago. The skeleton, estimated to be between 10,000 and 13,000 years old, was named Leanderthal Lady because of the proximity to nearby Leander, and hers is one of the earliest intact burials ever excavated in America. There is a highway historical marker at Farm Road 1431 commemorating the find.

. . . And Definitely the Largest Flying Animal Ever . . .

The Texas Memorial Museum in Austin (on Trinity Street) is home to the largest flying animal in the world. There you can view the remains of a pterosaur, with a wingspan of more than 40 feet! Don't worry, there are no pterosaurs anymore: Like all the other dinosaurs, pterosaurs became extinct about 65 million years ago.

Millions for the Finding: The Legend of Karl Steinheimer's Gold

This story involves a pirate, travel, a gold mine, some mules, a brass spike, several million dollars in gold—and a woman. It begins not in Texas or even in the United States but in Germany, with a young, unhappy boy. The legend of Karl's Steinheimer's gold goes something like this:

Eleven-year-old Karl Steinheimer was most likely

on a mission to find adventure, for at this tender age he left home and signed on with a merchant ship sailing out of Hamburg. His travels as a merchant marine took him all over the world—and imbued him with a fascination for piracy.

Around the time of the War of 1812, he fell in with a gang of pirates in Galveston, where, legend has it, a struggle ensued between Steinheimer and the famous pirate Jean Lafitte. The German merchant-marine-turned-pirate lost the bid for gang boss and worked his way aboard riverboats to St. Louis, Missouri, where he turned over a new leaf and also fell in love—hard. Proposing to the young lass, whose name is not recorded, she at first agreed to young Karl's proposal but then balked.

Heartbroken, Karl wondered what to do next. He found an answer in Mexico. Gold was there for the taking, everyone said, so off he went, settling in the state of Nuevo León as a mine owner. His mine was indeed extremely productive, and after 20 years, Karl was still young—and very, very wealthy.

One day he was sitting in a cantina and struck up a conversation with an American. Eventually the conversation turned to St. Louis, and the American said, yes, he knew of the woman Karl asked about—and she had never married. Karl was stunned, and it occurred to him that perhaps she had turned down his marriage proposal because he had had two strikes against him then: He was an ex-pirate and he was poor.

He was inspired: He'd show up in St. Louis with all of his wealth, and his love would then agree to become his bride! He liquidated all his land holdings, loaded 10 pack mules with all of his gold, hired a handful of Mexicans to escort him, and left Mexico for Missouri.

The good luck he'd had for the past two decades dissolved into tragedy once he crossed the Texas border: He came across throngs of Mexicans heading south. Texans, they told him and his entourage, were forcing anyone who was not a Texan to leave—the Texas War of Independence was at hand and Santa Anna and his Mexican Army were on the march toward San Antonio. After 20 years of living as a Mexican citizen, he was not safe.

Karl had to make a decision, and quickly. He decided to bury his gold, then ride alone to Missouri. He dismissed all but two of his most trusted Mexican helpers, and they began to dig. They had just finished burying all the gold beneath an oak tree and marking it with a brass stake when they were set upon by marauding Indians. The two Mexicans were killed, and Karl was wounded.

Karl evaded the Indians before they could kill him, hiding in a ravine for days. Sometime later, traveling Texans found him, wandering in the wilderness, with a festering wound. He knew he was dying and asked the travelers to take a last letter to a "relative."

The relative was not a relative but his lost love, still unmarried in St. Louis. And the letter was not a farewell letter but a map showing her where the gold could be found. The Texans left Karl dying but took his letter to be mailed.

Eventually, the letter/map made its way to Karl's love. After Texas won its independence from Mexico and things were settled down a bit, she hired a group of men to search for Karl's millions of dollars in buried gold.

The gold has never been found. Somewhere, just east of Interstate 35, about 10 miles north of Holland (which is near Temple), off Texas Highway 95 near the Little River, is Karl's gold—still buried.

Strange But True!

Trader or Terrorist?

In 1848, after the Mexican War, a frontiersman named Ben Leaton settled in the area now known as Presidio, on the present-day Texas–Mexico border. He settled in what was a strategic site, on the trail people took to get from Chihuahua, Mexico, to San Antonio, and right beside the Rio Grande River. Leaton saw a great opportunity in this arid land—to make a good living by taking advantage of the diverse traffic.

He began to trade with the Native Americans in the area and furnished supplies to traveling U.S. Army soldiers on patrol. Though he was accused of doing more than this—specifically, trading arms and ammunition to local tribespeople for stolen cattle and encouraging the local Native Americans to lead raids on settlements on the other side of the border—none of this was ever proven.

Leaton did make a fortune, and a name, for himself and eventually constructed a huge adobe fortress. Today, that fortress is known as Fort Leaton State Historic Site and is one of the most-photographed forts in the state.

Whether he was truly an honest, simple trader or a man who became wealthy through the accumulation of stolen property and terrorism will never be known for sure.

The Other Republic

In January of 1840, the southern town of Laredo became the capital of a republic that broke away from Mexico. Dubbed the Republic of the Rio Grande, it was short-lived, lasting a mere 283 days before being reclaimed by the Mexican Army.

Of course, you know the Republic of Texas was formed earlier—in 1836—but when it attempted to claim Laredo and the surrounding area as part of its republic (the Republic of Texas), the town's citizens refused, claiming loyalty to Mexico.

It took the 1848 Treaty of Guadalupe Hidalgo for the citizens of Laredo and the surrounding area (the former republic) to become part of the United States (which, by then, included the other former republic).

The Ghost Lights of Marfa

At dusk, in the desert around the Chianti Mountains of West Texas, you can view the lights that continue to defy explanation. More than 100 years ago, Apaches in the area had their own legend—that these lights that appeared near dark and floated around in no particular pattern were the ghosts of their ancestors. Later, settlers saw the lights and wrote down what they saw in journals and letters as early as the 1880s. Not too long ago, experts from the TV show Unsolved Mysteries checked out the lights to try to determine the cause, to no avail.

There are all kinds of theories about the causes of the lights, including car headlights (which didn't exist long ago) and the luminescent fur of desert animals. Some even say that the lights are the ghost of Mexican bandit Pancho Villa.

Whatever the cause of the lights, there is now a viewing center in the city of Marfa where you can go and see them for yourself.

The Oldest Community in Texas—Moved by a River!

A few miles east of El Paso is the community of Ysleta, which was established in 1682 by settlers and a group of Native Americans now known as the Tiwa. It is only in

Texas now, though, because years ago the Rio Grande River shifted its course—and instead of being a part of Mexico, the pueblo village found itself within the boundaries of Texas!

You can tour the mission, Nuestra Señora del Carmen, and the pueblo itself, visit the museum run by the Tiwa people, eat at a restaurant there, watch them make traditional breads in their huge bread ovens, and, on occasion, watch them dance on the plaza.

Remember the Alamo!

The Alamo had humble beginnings, and when in 1718 Franciscan missionaries built and named it Mission San Antonio de Valero, they surely had no idea to what importance the mission would become in the annals of American history.

Soldiers took over the Alamo when the missionaries left it in the 1790s. It may have gotten its name from the nearby cottonwood trees—Alamo means "cottonwood" in Spanish.

In 1836, Lieutenant Colonel William Barret Travis was commanding officer of the Alamo garrison. Sam Houston, in command of the Texas Army, had ordered a soldier named Colonel James Neill to destroy the Alamo and bring its 20 cannons to the Brazos River, where he was trying to raise an army against the Mexicans. Santa Anna's Mexican Army had been defeated in 1835, and the infamous dictator was about to launch another offensive to attempt to recapture Texas.

Colonel James Bowie told Neill to ignore Houston's orders—they would make their stand not at the Brazos River but at the Alamo herself. (The now-famous Bowie probably felt that he had little to lose—he had fled to Texas from Louisiana in a legal entanglement over some unscrupulous land deals.) They reasoned that San Antonio de Bexar, as the town was named back then, was the only important town in West Texas at the time, and that Texas should be defended at that point.

The 140 men at the Alamo rallied around Davy Crockett, who arrived with his dozen or so Tennessee Mounted Volunteers to help defend the Alamo against Santa Anna's thousands of soldiers. On February 23, 1836, from the steeple of San Fernando Church, Santa Anna's soldiers raised a flag the color of fresh blood—a sign meaning that they intended to take no prisoners. They then bombarded the mission for 24 hours.

In answer, Crockett played tunes on his fiddle loud enough for Santa Anna's men to hear, and the men of the Alamo cut loose their largest cannon, an 18-pounder. The thunder that it made was a defiant challenge: "Come and get us!"

Meanwhile, messengers had been sent by Travis to the nearby garrison of Goliad, Fort Defiance, and to Gonzales. Only Gonzales sent their 32 soldiers to come to the aid of the Alamo (all volunteered save one, who fled). Led by the messengers (Dr. John Sutherland and John W. Smith), they arrived at the Alamo on March 1, slipping through the Mexican lines.

Travis sent Smith on another foray, this time with more pleas for help from Texas. When Smith left this time, he also carried farewell letters from the soldiers to their loved ones back home. The night of March 5, Travis is said to have drawn a line in the dust and told anyone who wanted to leave, and live, that they could do so, but as for him, it was victory or death. Only one man—Louis Rose, formerly a French trader—fled rather than fight.

The next day, Santa Anna's army attacked the Alamo on all sides, by the hundreds, against the handful of

Texas soldiers and volunteer soldiers. You know the rest of the story—in the battle, which lasted 1½ hours, nearly all of the defenders had been killed, as opposed to approximately 200 Mexicans killed and about 400 wounded. Bowie, stricken with what is now thought to be typhoid pneumonia, was killed in his sickbed. (Dr. John Shackelford was spared because he could be useful to the Mexicans; Shackelford County is named in his honor.)

The half dozen or so surviving defenders were then taken before Santa Anna by General Manuel Fernández Castrillón, who had promised these men that they would be fairly treated by the dictator. To Castrillon's horror, Santa Anna ordered his soldiers to hack the survivors to death. One of the soldiers to die this way was Davy Crockett. The bodies of those who had died in the Alamo battle and those hacked to death were stacked between layers of bushwood and burned. Historical accounts of the aftermath of the massacre quote Santa Anna as saying, as he walked among his own wounded soldiers, "These are the chickens. Much blood has been shed, but the battle is over. It was but a small affair."

That's about all most people remember, and most people think that there were no survivors save Smith, the messenger. However, there had been approximately 20 women and children in the Alamo at the time of the battle; they had huddled in the chapel and were spared. One of the survivors was a woman named Susannah Dickinson, the young wife of Captain Almeron Dickinson, who had been the Alamo's artillery officer. She related later that Travis had come to the women and children on the eve of battle. He had spoken to the women, preparing them for the battle to come, and had given the children some trinkets and gifts. He also slipped a cat's-eye ring from his finger, placing it on a string and tying it around the neck of

Dickinson's 15-month-old daughter, Angela.

Sam Houston met the young widow and her young daughter in Gonzales on March 15, when he learned of the Alamo's fate. He also learned that Santa Anna's soldiers had attacked Goliad's Fort Defiance and that after those soldiers surrendered, Santa Anna had ordered them all shot.

With patriotic vengefulness in his heart, Houston rallied his troops near the Brazos River while Santa Anna divided his soldiers in an attempt to scatter and crush any resistance. Finally Houston and his men attacked Santa Anna at Buffalo Bayou on the San Jacinto River in what is known today as The Battle of San Jacinto.

Crying out, "Remember the Alamo! Remember Goliad!" the Texas soldiers fought, bolstered by the courage of those who had died for their freedom, and all accounts agree that each man fought with the ferocity of 10 men. The odds were once again stacked against the Texans—1,500 Texans to 5,800 Mexicans—but Houston and his army killed approximately 600 Mexican soldiers and captured all of the rest, losing only 8 of their own men, with 23 Texans sustaining wounds.

This battle lasted only 18 minutes, and Santa Anna was held captive until his government granted independence to Texas in the fall of 1836. The Lone Star Republic voted Sam Houston its first president.

Today when you visit the Alamo, the air still seems alive with the heroic spirit of the men who died defending Texas freedom. Other places in Texas also serve as reminders of this time of Texas's trial by fire: In Waco at the Texas Ranger Hall of Fame and Museum (see below to learn more about the Texas Rangers), you can see Santa Anna's sword, and the San Jacinto Battleground State Historic Site in Deer Park commemorates the avenging of the Alamo defeat and the winning of Texas's independence from Mexico.

Also, on the main plaza in San Antonio, remains that are believed to be those of some of the heroes of the Alamo are interred near the entryway of San Fernando Church. A plaque there reads: "Here lie the remains of Travis, Crockett, Bowie, and other Alamo Heroes." Stephen F. Austin, the "Father of Texas," is remembered in a number of places, including a beautiful statue in San Felipe.

Sam Houston is revered throughout the state, especially in the town of Huntsville, which has Sam Houston State University, a statue of him on the grounds, and a mural honoring his memory. There is also a memorial museum complex there, which sprawls across 15 acres and includes eight buildings and loads of artifacts relating to the many victories of Houston's life. The complex hosts the General Sam Houston Folk Festival every April. Just outside the city of Huntsville is the Sam Houston National Forest.

The San Fernando Church, from which Santa Anna raised his "take no prisoners" blood-red flag, just before the battle of the Alamo. Courtesy, San Antonio Convention and Visitors Bureau.

In the days of the struggle for Texas independence, the phrase "Remember the Alamo!" was a call for courage and gallantry against nearly impossible odds. Now, nearly 200 years later, that phrase is still a call to fight for freedom, whatever the cost.

This Just In . . . Crockett's Last Letter

Just two months prior to the battle of the Alamo and his heroic death, Davy Crockett wrote a letter to his daughter and son-in-law. In the letter, Crockett described Texas as the "garden spot of the world . . . the best land . . . ," with optimal prospects for any ambitious, hardworking settler such as himself.

Fast-forward from then to the recent past, when a man by the name of Simpson purchased the letter from a descendant of Crockett's, then misplaced it. The letter remained missing for years, then in the fall of 2007 was rediscovered by Simpson's grandson, Ray, and his father.

In September of that year, Ray Simpson decided, rather than auction the letter, to offer it to the state of Texas first. Texas purchased the letter from Ray, owner of Simpson Galleries, which is Houston's oldest fine arts auctioneer. At a ceremony held at the Bob Bullock Texas State History Museum, Governor Rick Perry accepted the letter on behalf of the citizens of the Lone Star State.

Plans are now being made to display the letter, the last known communication from Crockett to his family. Thanks to Ray Simpson, an important piece in the story of Texas's past has found a home.

The Story of the Texas Rangers

Long known for being tough and effective, the Texas Rangers were organized in 1823 by Stephen F. Austin. In those days, settlers were attacked by all kinds of aggressive people—robbers, hostile Native Americans, and highway bandits—and needed some sort of protection.

Originally called "ranging companies," the first company consisted of only 10 men. Men who wanted to become a Texas Ranger had to, in the words of author Rachel Barenblat (Texas: The Lone Star State, World Almanac Library of the States series), "ride like a Mexican, track like a Comanche, shoot like a Kentuckian, and fight like the devil." Someone going up against a Ranger was said to be either foolish or had a death wish, for they always "got their man."

Today, there are more than 100 Texas Rangers, and these men and women work alongside other law-enforcement personnel such as sheriffs and police. In Waco, you can visit the Texas Ranger Hall of Fame and Museum (located at 100 Texas Ranger Trail), which honors and commemorates the efforts of the heroes who are known for their signature white hats. Texas Rangers and their long-standing reputation for no-nonsense upholding of the law have been portrayed in numerous movies, documentaries, and TV series (such as Walker, Texas Ranger). They're still around, still a force to reckon with. And still nobody messes with 'em.

Petroglyphs in the Panhandle: Alibates National Monument

In the panhandle region of Texas—the northern "handle" of Texas bordered to the north and east by Oklahoma and to the west by New Mexico—is a geographic monument to the past, an area that contains a part of Texas history shared by no other area in the state.

In the phase of history archeologists call the Antelope Creek phase (roughly 1150–1450 ad), a prehistoric culture of people thrived whom experts say had no written form of communication. Believed by some to have originated from the Mississippian Woodlands peoples, the people of the Antelope Creek culture lived in elevated dwellings, led an agrarian lifestyle, obtained flint (a mineral that was hard enough to create sparks and therefore start fires) from nearby Alibates and Plum creeks, made pottery and other items such as pipes, and participated in a democratic community very similar to the current U.S. system.

Scenes of the Alibates Monument. Courtesy Randall Derrick/National Park Service. Used with permission.

Alibates flint can best be described as a multicolored stone that not only is beautiful but also can hold a sharp edge. The people of this region mined and used alibates in a number of ingenious ways. The place where they mined flint has been made into a tourable site called the Alibates Flint Quarries National Monument, consisting of 736 quarry pits located within the park. Located just northeast of Amarillo, the site is of archeological importance because of the many items that have been found here—tools, pottery, beads, and stonework.

Something else that is found nowhere else in Texas but the Panhandle are rock carvings. Also known as petroglyphs, these rock carvings, formed in dolomite, have been found here and in portions of New Mexico and Oklahoma. The carvings are often of footprints, buffalo, turtles, and other animals. Dolomite was probably carved using a crude, chisel-type instrument made from either quartzite or flint. Using the chisel and another tool for a hammer, the carver created images that have survived centuries.

Although some scientists have, as mentioned earlier, said that this was a culture with no written form of communication, further investigation of the petroglyphs makes one wonder if this is true.

To find out more, I contacted Randall Derrick, editor of the electronic magazine Panhandle Nation (at www. panhandlenation.com) and a longtime explorer of and researcher at the Alibates Flint Quarries National Monument. He was kind enough to give me his observations, which leads to amazing, intriguing suggestions as to the far-reaching abilities of this vanished culture.

First, he explained, the carved stones are arranged in a kind of gallery at the monument site, about 100 yards west of the site of the former dwellings, on a cliff above the river breaks, creating something of an amphitheater. Arranged in a shape resembling a 90-degree curve with the open side of the arc facing south, first there are two stones with turtle petroglyphs on them, followed by another with a bison (buffalo), a large footprint, and another with what must have once more closely resembled a man. The man has his arms held above his head. Both of the heads of the two turtle carvings face north—but there's more.

The turtle on the left side points to about 279 degrees north by northwest, and the one on the right points to about 289 or 290 degrees north by northwest. Phillips ventured a guess about the meaning and/or utility of this placement: "One wonders if the turtles were purposely placed to generally face the northern direction or to face toward the river or perhaps in some relationship to a certain astronomical object [such as the Big Dipper] or event."

Did the Antelope Creek people know of astronomical measurements and the placement of the stars and have mathematic skills to enable them to create drawings with such possible meaning? We can only venture a guess, for the people of this period disappeared under mysterious circumstances shortly after 1400 ad.

You can visit the Alibates Flint Quarries National Monument and see the petroglyphs for yourself. You can also see and learn more about the area and its ancient peoples. Maybe you can help solve the mystery of the Antelope Creek culture, their strange carvings, and what happened to them.

Before Texans Were Texans: the Alabama-Coushatta Tribe's History

There are approximately 4,600 acres of forested land in Polk County, near Livingston. This is the current home to 550 members of the Alabama-Coushatta tribe, who made their home in what is now Texas, before it was Texas—way back in the late 1700s.

At first two separate tribes, these members of the Creek Confederacy were discovered long ago by Spanish explorer Hernando de Soto, circa 1541. At that time they were living in what is now central Mississippi. Becoming well established along the banks of the Alabama River, the name began to be applied to the tribe as well as the yet-to-be state of Alabama.

Pushed out of these homelands by encroaching settlers, the Alabamas entered what is now Texas in the late 1700s and early 1800s; the Coushattas arrived about the same time. Although the newly forming Texas government was then earnestly removing other Native American tribes, such as the Caddo (who were expelled to Oklahoma), from the state, Congress granted land for these indigenous people in 1840. There was a reason for this favor: The tribespeople had fought alongside Texans in the War of Independence against Mexico. The gesture was one of gratitude.

The feeling of gratitude didn't last long, however, and demanding settlers disputed the claims of the Alabama-Coushatta, driving away the Native Americans and taking the land for themselves. In stepped hero and President Sam Houston, who returned the land to the tribespeople, and in 1854 the Alabama-Coushatta finally had a permanent place to call home. In the next century, the tribe began to pursue legislation to become federally recognized, finally receiving this designation in 1987.

In keeping with their native philosophies, the Alabama-Coushatta people make every decision as to how, in their words, it will effect "seven generations back and seven generations forward." For tourists and interested travelers, the tribe has a museum with a reconstructed traditional village and gives train rides through the Big Thicket National Preserve. They also have a restaurant offering traditional native dishes.

After your visit, you can say that you have been to Texas's oldest Native American reservation.

Q & A

Q. What town bills itself as "The Best of the Border" and, among its other attractions, has more than 400 archeological sites, including cave paintings?

A. The city of Del Rio, in Big Bend Country, just over the border from Mexico. Del Rio has more cave paintings and pictographs than virtually any other city in the United States.

Q. What, in Odessa, is 550 feet in diameter, originally was 100 feet deep, and was created during prehistoric times?

A. The Odessa Crater, which was formed by a shower of meteorites

Q. What Spanish explorer is said to be the first European to explore the area that is now known as Corpus Christi?

A. Alonzo Álvarez de Pineda, in 1519.

Q. What artifact lies on display in the Rankin Museum in Rankin, Texas, in connection with the crater?

A. A fragment of a meteorite, believed to be one that struck Odessa and created the crater there

Q. What town, established in 1824, was first known as Macaroni Station, and why?

A. The town of Edna served as a commissary for the workers of the New York, Texas and Mexican Railway. The workers were predominantly Italian, and the word macaroni was once commonly used as a slur against Italians.

Q. In what town are said to be the best-preserved dinosaur tracks in the state?

A. Glen Rose, the site of Dinosaur Valley State Park.

FAMOUS TEXANS

DID YOU KNOW?

Our Hoss

Dan Blocker, a star in the Western TV series Bonanza who is fondly remembered as "Hoss" Cartwright, grew up in O'Donnell. The city of O'Donnell honors his memory with a bust of him, complete with broad smile and cowboy hat, and much of the memorabilia in the O'Donnell Museum is related to Blocker's life.

Lonesome Larry

Larry McMurtry, the well-loved author of the Western Lonesome Dove and other novels, was born in Archer City.

"Best Little Bordello Museum in Texas"

Miss Hattie's Bordello Museum in San Angelo is fondly known as the "Best Little Bordello Museum in Texas." Miss Hattie and her "girls" were part and parcel of the culture of the West from the mid-1880s until she was forced out of business by the Texas Rangers in 1946. You can tour the museum, which looks much as it did when Miss Hattie's business was booming.

The most interesting thing about this particular museum, though, is that it's available for you to rent overnight! Hmmm.

First Gowns

You can see the actual inaugural gowns worn by the First Ladies of Texas at an exhibit in Denton, on the campus of Texas Women's University.

The Man Who "Never Met a Man He Didn't Like"

Originally born in the Cherokee Nation (part of Oklahoma), in 1879, the man the world knew as Will Rogers learned how to lasso so well that he was entered in the Guinness World Records for throwing three lassoes at once. He became a humorist, philosopher, Broadway actor, and movie star (of more than 71 movies in the 1920s and 1930s). He also wrote six novels and newspaper columns and traveled internationally. He is best known for saying, "I never met a man I didn't like."

He died in a plane crash in Alaska in 1935 and is honored as the preeminent cowboy humorist at the Will Rogers Memorial Center in Fort Worth.

Chipping Her Way into Fame

Well-known German sculptress Elizabet Ney (who immigrated to Texas in the 1870s) had a studio in Austin. The studio is now the Elizabet Ney Museum and has been made into a National Historic Site. Although her work is exhibited in palaces in Europe and in the Smithsonian American Art Museum (including other places), the largest collection of her work is here.

Ney was not buried in Austin, however. She lies beside her husband, Dr. Edmond Montgomery, on the grounds of the Liendo Plantation in Hempstead. Like the museum in Austin, Liendo Plantation is on the National Register of Historic Places, and both are open for tours.

The Short List of Famous Texans

You will find other famous Texans in separate chapters (for example, Frank Robinson is in chapter 7, "Sports Stories"). This is only a partial list—and more Texans become famous every day!

Famous Texans Matching Game

See if you can match the description with the person (answers below, but don't peek!).

a. Mary Martin	b. Larry Hagman
c. Jimmy Dean	d. Dan Jenkins
e. Jessica Simpson	f. Ramsey Clark
g. James A. Baker III	h. Tommy Lee Jones
i. Debbie Allen	j. Phylicia Rashad
k. Patrick Swayze	l. Sissy Spacek
m. Zachary Scott	n. Randy Quaid
o. Dennis Quaid	p. Phyllis George
q. Rip Torn	r. Farrah Fawcett
s. Sam Donaldson	t. Joan Crawford
u. Dan Rather	w. Howard Hughes

1. Country music singer and owner of a well-known sausage trademark

2. Former secretary of the treasury, 1985–1988, and secretary of state 1898–1993; born in Houston

3. Broadway star, best known for playing the lead role in Peter Pan; a statue of Peter Pan honors this actor in Weatherford

4. Probably best known for his book, Semi-Tough, and for his column in Golf Digest; lives in Fort Worth

5.   U.S. attorney general

6.   Born in 1952 in Houston; his mother was a chore-ographer. An actor and dancer, he received a Golden Globe nomination for his role as the dance instructor Johnny Castle in the movie Dirty Dancing, starring opposite Jennifer Grey.

7.   Actor born in San Saba, Texas, in 1946. Starred opposite Sissy Spacek in Coal Miner's Daughter as Loretta Lynn's husband Doolittle, one of the movies for which he is best known.

8.   Houston native and actress probably best known for her role as Claire Huxtable in the TV series The Cosby Show.

9.   Native of Dallas tried out for the Mickey Mouse Club but was turned down; married singer Nick Lachey and starred with her husband in the TV reality series Newlyweds—until their divorce

10.   Best known for his role of J.R. Ewing in the TV series Dallas

11.   Born in Houston in 1950, sister to Phylicia Rashad, dancer, choreographer, actress, and movie producer, this woman starred as the dance teacher in the movie Fame and produced Steven Spielberg's movie Amistad.

12.   Born in 1914 in Austin, he died of a malignant brain tumor in 1965. Played either very sinister or very smooth leading men; best known for his role in The Southerner in 1945.

13.   Born in Houston (1954); appeared in the movies Breaking Away (1979) and The Alamo (2004). Is also a musician—plays with a band called the Sharks—and used to be married to Meg Ryan.

14.   Born in Houston (1950); played the role of Doc Holliday in the movie Purgatory (1999) and of Joe Aguirre in

Brokeback Mountain.

15. Born in 1949 in Quitman, Texas, she was a homecoming queen at her high school, which was much like her role in one of her earliest movies—Carrie, in 1976. Has frequently acted opposite Tommy Lee Jones. Given name was Mary Elizabeth.

16. Born in Temple in 1931; first name at birth was Elmore. Starred in Sweet Bird of Youth; is commissioner of Extreme Dodgeball League.

17. Born in San Antonio in 1905 under the birth name Lucille Fay LeSueur; acting name was the result of a contest; probably best known for her role opposite Bette Davis in Whatever Happened to Baby Jane? (1962); was the subject of the movie Mommy Dearest.

18. Born in 1934 in El Paso, he was ABC's chief White House correspondent from 1977 until 1989.

19. One of the original cast members of Charlie's Angels; born in Corpus Christi in 1947; at one time was married to actor Lee Majors.

20. Television commentator, born in Denton in 1949, was a beauty contestant in her earlier years; was crowned Miss Texas in 1970 and Miss America in 1971

21. CBS News anchor and native of Wharton

22. What Texas-born Renaissance man with the Midas touch was a groundbreaking aviator, film producer and director, and, at the time of his death in 1976, was one of the wealthiest men in the world (hint: he made Jane Russell famous in the "banned" movie, The Outlaw)?

Answers: 1, c; 2, g; 3, a; 4, d; 5, f; 6, k; 7, h; 8, j; 9, e; 10, b; 11, i; 12, m; 13, o; 14, n; 15, l; 16, q; 17, t; 18, s; 19, r; 20, p; 21, u; 22, w

We Have a Weak Spot for Dog Stories

Everybody loves a dog story, and that's why Fred Gipson, author of <u>Old Yeller</u> (among other works), was so popular. He made his home in Mason, Texas; there is a very nice exhibit relating to Gipson and his life and works located in the Mason County M. Beven Eckert Memorial Library.

A Tribute to the Wives of Texas Presidents

First of all, for those who are confused as to why this topic is not in chapter 2, "Politics, Transportation, and Military Tales," here is an explanation: The women written about below were larger-than-life people, and regardless of who they'd married, they would have made a difference in the world. They are therefore in this chapter dealing with famous Texans, politics aside.

In the movie My Big Fat Greek Wedding, the mother of the bride-to-be explains to her daughter a woman's role: "The man," she says, "is the head of the house. But the woman is the neck—and she can turn the head any way she wants."

Turning the heads of U.S. presidents, particularly those from Texas, couldn't have been easy. In tribute to those women who stood by their men and helped make their presidencies memorable, I offer these brief biographies.

Mamie Eisenhower

Born Mamie Geneva Doud on November 14, 1896, in Boone, Iowa, she attended Mulholland School in San Antonio while the family spent their winters there. While staying with friends at Fort Sam Houston in 1915, the young debutante met her future husband, Dwight D. Eisenhower, who was born in Denison, Texas. He was a recent West

Point graduate, and her engagement ring was a smaller replica of his class ring.

They married in 1916, and their first home was a two-room apartment at Fort Sam Houston. They lived on less then $162 per month. The young bride recalled in a later memoir (Mrs. Ike, by Susan Eisenhower) that her husband taught her to cook.

Women get steel in their spines through hardship, and Mamie was no exception. She lost her first child (Doud Dwight Eisenhower, nicknamed "Ikky") at the tender age of three to meningitis caused by scarlet fever. Their second son, John Sheldon Doud Eisenhower, was born in 1922, which helped to heal the scar left by Ikky's death.

Her husband's military career found Mamie traveling the world, from various posts in the United States to the Panama Canal Zone and Europe. During World War II, when her husband was a general, Mamie eschewed the media, choosing to devote her time and energies to doing volunteer work, much of it for the Red Cross. After the war, with her husband serving as supreme allied commander of NATO forces, Mamie lived in Paris.

In 1952, she campaigned by her husband's side when he ran for president, and that same year, she made the Gallup Poll's Ten Most Admired Women in America. She served as First Lady until 1961.

The woman who gave the United States a model of self-sacrifice and gentility passed away in 1979 and is buried beside Ike and their firstborn son in the Place of Meditation at the Eisenhower Center, located in Abilene, Kansas. Dwight is honored at the Eisenhower Birthplace State Historic Site in Denison.

Lady Bird Johnson

Born Claudia Alta Taylor in Karnack, Texas, in 1912, Lady Bird Johnson was the daughter of a general-store owner. Her mother passed away when the child was only five, and an aunt (Effie Pattillo) came to care for her. The nickname "Lady Bird" is said to have been given to her by a nursemaid, who stated that little Claudia was "as pretty as a lady bird." The name stuck throughout her life.

All of Lady Bird's education was in Texas, from grammar school in Harrison County to her college years at the University of Texas. After earning a degree in journalism in 1934, that same year she married Texas native Lyndon Baines Johnson, after a brief courtship. During their long marriage, they had two daughters: Lynda Bird and Luci Baines.

In 1937, when Johnson campaigned successfully for a seat with the House of representatives, Lady Bird was his helpmate. She kept the home fires burning, caring for their two children while Johnson served in the navy during World War II, and then was his sounding board when he went on to serve the public interest first in the House of Representatives and then, in 1953, in the Senate.

When he ran as John F. Kennedy's vice-presidential candidate, Lady Bird was his strongest supporter. On the terrible night of November 22, 1963, after Kennedy was assassinated, she stood by and watched as her husband took the oath as the leader of the nation. Exhorting the country's people to aspire to build a "great society," he captured America's imagination with his wife's support, and when he ran for president again in 1964, he won by a 61 percent margin of the vote.

America's love for Lady Bird contributed to her husband's success in leading the country through those years. With her at his side, he took visionary steps to beautify the country, eradicate ignorance, and care for the poor (Medicare was begun then). No one was more interested in these things than Lady Bird Johnson herself: During her years in the White House, she served as honorary chairperson of the national Head Start program and received numerous awards and honors for her work to make America a more beautiful (and educated) place. One act that she pushed for, for example, was the Highway Beautification Act of 1965.

After Johnson withdrew his bid to run again for the presidency (because of the strain of the Vietnam War), Mrs. Johnson penned two books: <u>A White House Diary</u> (of her memoirs in her years there) and <u>Wildflowers Across America</u> (coauthored by Carlton Lees).

Lyndon Johnson passed away at their LBJ Ranch in Texas on January 22, 1973. She outlived him until July 2007, and the busy world paused to lay to rest a lady of grace, beauty, and inspiration. Gardens throughout the state, particularly the 42-acre Lady Bird Johnson Wildflower Center in Austin, bear her name and honor her memory.

Barbara Bush

Barbara Pierce, born in New York in 1925, met Massachusetts-born George Herbert Walker Bush just before he went off to war, when she was 16. They married in 1945. He went on to be a World War II navy pilot and then a Texas oilman. Like Mamie Eisenhower, Barbara Bush also experienced the loss of a child (her daughter Robin), but the disease involved was leukemia. The family grew after this, however, and came to include four sons and a daughter.

Barbara Bush has always maintained a sense of grace, dignity, and priorities despite the whirlwind of being in the limelight through the years when her husband served as first as representative to Congress from Texas, then later as ambassador to the United Nations, chairman of the Republican National Committee, and other high offices (such as director of the CIA). In 1980, her husband became the vice-president, and then in 1988, the president of the country, making her the First Lady until 1992.

I came across an interesting anecdote about Barbara Bush's personality while researching her life. While helping her husband campaign for president, she cut her ankle while ascending a stage before he began speaking to a waiting crowd. Instead of calling attention to herself, she refused medical aid for the cut (which required more than half a dozen stitches) until her husband had finished his speech.

Now, although she is no longer First Lady in the White House, Barbara Bush continues to be First Lady in the hearts of many Americans, and for good reason. The name Barbara Bush is synonymous with doing for others and creating a better world, and in serving this cause, she has worked with hundreds of philanthropic causes and social services. She's a longtime supporter of the Leukemia & Lymphoma Society, the Boys & Girls Clubs of America, and the Ronald McDonald House (the latter of which offers parents of cancer patients a place to stay while their children are receiving oncology treatment).

One of her main accomplishments continues to be in the realm of literacy, and in 1989 she formed the Barbara Bush Foundation for Family Literacy, to help wipe out illiteracy and its societal ills related to it. One of the most charming things she did related to literacy was reading stories aloud on a radio show entitled Mrs. Bush's Story Time.

Barbara Bush has penned three books: C. Fred's Story, Barbara Bush: A Memoir, and Millie's Book (the latter written while she was in the White House and "coauthored" by her dog Millie). Still active in charitable and humanitarian circles, Barbara Bush continues to inspire Americans everywhere—and to fill Texans with pride.

Laura Bush

Laura Bush was born Laura Welch in Midland in 1946. One of her early teachers inspired her to set her sights on education, and toward that goal, she earned a degree in education from Southern Methodist University in 1968. After teaching for a while in Dallas and Houston, she returned to school herself, to earn a degree in library science from the University of Texas. In 1977, she met and married the son of George Herbert Walker Bush, Texas-raised George Walker Bush. Together, they had twin daughters, Barbara and Jenna (named for their grandmothers). Laura Bush was First Lady of Texas when her husband became governor in 1994, then stood by his side as he again took that oath of office in 1998.

Since in 2001 George Bush followed in his father's presidential footsteps, Laura Bush has found many outlets for her vision to make improvements in the areas of human rights, basic health care, and especially education. Like her mother-in-law, she too has been a spokesperson for literacy and education, working with groups such as Teach for America and Troops to Teachers (a program whereby soldiers leaving the military are offered training and incentives to teach), and launching the initial National Book Festival (working with the Library of Congress), which was held in September 2001 in Washington, D.C. She has been named honorary ambassador for a literacy program begun by the United Nations and in that capacity has served as their international spokesperson. Like Lady Bird Johnson, she loves natural beauty, and she helped found Preserve America, a project to protect both aesthetic attractions in the country as well we preserve treasures of our heritage.

There will be other First Ladies to come from the Lone Star state—and maybe eventually, a Texas woman will be president.

He Was What All the Buzz Was About

In the late 1800s, Alabama-born visionary physician William C. Gorgas contracted a deadly disease: the dreaded yellow fever. A highly contagious disease, it is carried by mosquitoes, something not known then. The illness has a sudden onset and renders the victim prostrate, with high fever, headache, jaundice, and sometimes hemorrhaging. Most of its victims died—and were happy to do so.

The black-and-white, oval picture with a man in the middle is of Dr. Gorgas. Courtesy, the digital collection, Freshwater and Marine Image Bank Repository.

Dr. Gorgas didn't die. It was early in his army career and he was young and quite healthy, and he recovered. He began to study the disease that had almost caused his demise, conducting experiments on how mosquitoes might transmit yellow fever. He also began searching for preventative measures, continuing to do so when he was sent to Fort Brown, Texas, appointed to the U.S. Army Medical Corps, in 1880. When Dr. Walter Reed announced his discovery that yellow fever was caused by disease-carrying mosquitoes, Dr. Gorgas knew that his suspicions were right, and in 1898 he was sent to U.S.-occupied Cuba to begin sanitation measures to eradicate yellow fever there.

He set to work getting rid of mosquito-breeding spots at the camp in Havana (Siboney) and was so successful in eradicating the disease from the city that he became famous in international medical circles. In 1904, when construction began on the Panama Canal, Dr. Gorgas was sent there to head up sanitation and malaria-prevention measures there. History will forever record him as making completion of the Panama Canal possible, by keeping the workers healthy and able. He later achieved similar results in Ecuador and was named U.S. Surgeon General in 1914.

Today, when you visit Brownsville, you can visit Fort Brown, where Dr. Gorgas conducted many of his experiments. Now you know the irony of it all: had it not been for this man becoming deathly ill with a mosquito-borne disease, we might never have seen yellow fever and malaria eradicated—and the Panama Canal would not exist!

Before Luckenbach Was Made Famous by the Song . . .

The town of Luckenbach was put on the map by a real Texas character named Hondo Crouch. He died in 1976, but he remains legendary. He was dubbed the "Clown Prince of Luckenbach," for his great sense of humor—aimed toward others as well as himself. Always a visionary with a quirky playfulness, he inspired the people of Luckenbach toward the unusual, working to organize off-the-wall events such as all-female chili cook-offs.

His daughter, Becky Crouch Patterson, has written a book about the man Texas will remember as an entertainer, an authentic Texan with star quality. Oh, and by the way—he was the inspiration behind the song "Luckenbach, Texas," the hit sung by Willie Nelson and Waylon Jennings.

Hondo Crouch of Luckenbach Texas, who inspired the song. Courtesy Becky Crouch Patterson.

If you ever make it to Luckenbach, be prepared for spontaneous entertaining events they refer to there as "happenings," especially if it's a Sunday afternoon. Crouch's legend lives on.

Cal Farley's Legacy

Carl Farley was a Texas businessman and, prior to that, a world welterweight champion in the 1920s. He wanted to do something more, though, than have fame and fortune: He wanted to have a positive impact on troubled youth.

In 1939, Farley established Boys Ranch outside Amarillo, then later created Girlstown. More than 400 boys and girls every year have their lives turned around by this experience.

Boys Ranch is now a 11,000-acre operation, a village in itself. Every September, the organization has a rodeo, and more than 40 young people graduate from this life-changing place every year. Farley passed away in 1967 but is known by some as "America's Greatest Foster Father." His likeness is on a U.S. postage stamp, and the Amarillo Civic Center was renamed for Farley in 1989.

Texas's Original Renaissance Man

The state of Texas is full of people who excel at a myriad of endeavors, and this may be, in part anyway, because of the legacy left by Sam Houston. Born in Lexington, Virginia, in 1793, his mother took him and his siblings to Tennessee after the death of his father. He must not have been happy with his lot, for at the age of 15, young Houston ran away from home and went to live with a band of local Cherokee.

He was still living with the Cherokee when the War of 1812 broke out; Houston enlisted in the U.S. Army and, serving under Andrew Jackson, rose to the rank of lieutenant. Afterward, he took up the study of law and opened a law office in Nashville, Tennessee. He bid for, and won, a seat with the U.S. House of Representatives, serving in this capacity from 1823 until 1827, and then successfully ran for the office of governor of Tennessee.

He was briefly and unhappily married; when this relationship ended, Houston resigned as Tennessee's governor and once again lived with his beloved Cherokees, who named him Raven, after the bird prized for its intelligence and quickness of mind. He later protected the Cherokees' interests in Washington, D.C. and protesting injustices done to them.

Andrew Jackson, who was U.S. president in 1832, then commissioned Houston to work with indigenous tribes in Texas, negotiating treaties between those tribes and the U.S. government. (Texas still belonged to Mexico at the time, but U.S. hunters and traders sought the protection of their government against tribal hostilities.) Houston fell in love with Texas and its people and by 1835 was commander in chief of the Texas Army. His victory against Santa Anna after the Battle of San Jacinto not only wrought revenge for those who lost their lives at the Battle of the Alamo (see "Remember the Alamo!" in Chapter 3) but also won Texas her independence from Mexico.

Houston served as first president of the Republic of Texas from 1836 until 1838, then in 1841 was elected to that office again. Texas entered the Union in 1845, and Houston served as a U.S. Senator from 1846 to 1859, serving for a time as governor of Texas. In this capacity, he voiced his opposition to secession. In 1861, at the outbreak of the Civil War, Governor Houston refused to swear allegiance to the Confederate States of America and was stripped of his title. He died in Huntsville in July 1863.

Many monuments and other memorials continue to honor this Renaissance man, who was during his lifetime a teacher, lawyer, governor, president, soldier, and activist on behalf of Native Americans. The city of Houston is named after him, as is the Sam Houston State University in Huntsville, along with a myriad of parks, sporting arenas, and tourist attractions. In San Antonio, Fort Sam Houston has been recognized as a National Historic Landmark and has more historic structures (more than 900) of any other army installation in the world (it's also known as the "Home of Army Medicine").

Deep in the Heart of Texans

Born in Lake Charles, Louisiana, to Lebanese immigrants, one boy grew up to discover that he had a gift for healing others, a talent for medicine. In the early 1940s, after completing his medical studies at Tulane, he volunteered for the U.S. Army to help the war effort. During the war, he joined the staff of the U.S. Surgeon General and became chief of the Surgical Consultants Division. While in Europe, he inspected field hospitals, performed surgeries, and otherwise cared for the war wounded. His efforts ultimately led to the creation of MASH units, or Mobile Army Surgical Hospital units, and for his efforts he was awarded the Legion of Merit in 1945.

Following this, the physician was involved in cardiovascular (heart and circulatory system) surgeries and conducted groundbreaking research on the artificial heart. In 1966, the surgeon made medical history when he performed the first successful implantation of part of an artificial heart.

By the age of 98, the man known for his compassion, innovation, and vision had operated on more than 60,000 patients in Houston alone, earned the Presidential Medal of Freedom with Distinction, the American Legion Distinguished Service Award, the National Medal of Science, and more than 50 honorary degrees from medical schools and other higher institutions of learning across the United States.

In February 2007, Congressman Al Green introduced a bill to award the Congressional Gold Medal to the man you know as Dr. Michael E. DeBakey. The bill was enthusiastically supported by no less than 10 original co-sponsors, including Congressman John Culberson (Texas District 7) and Congressman Michael Burgess (Texas District 26). Burgess hailed Dr. DeBakey as "a legend in medical and humanitarian circles," and Green agreed, adding that Dr. DeBakey was known for how he treated his patients: "the very rich and the very poor . . . with the same high standards of care and unwavering compassion."

With a heart as big as Texas, a head full of knowledge, and gifted hands, Dr. DeBakey is a living example of what it means to make one's life extraordinary.

Be Careful What You Ask For

Raised in North Carolina, the son of a physician, the young man had an air of gentility. After his parents died, he moved to Texas, working first at a ranch, then as a bank teller at the First National Bank in Austin. Like many authors (or aspiring authors), the young man longed for one thing: to have a huge block of time in which to write.

Before long, the young teller got his wish, but not in the way he might have expected: He was charged with embezzlement! Fleeing the country (and leaving behind his sickly wife, Athol), he escaped to Honduras, because then it had no extradition treaty with the United States. In 1898, upon learning that Athol was deathly ill, he hastened back to Austin, where he was duly tried for the crime of embezzlement and sentenced to three years in an Ohio prison.

Convict 30664 carried with him such an air of dignity and good manners that inmates and prison guards alike agreed: This well-spoken gentleman didn't belong behind prison walls and iron bars. He served his time well and used it wisely, and for the first time in his life had that huge block of time to write for which he had so longed. During this time, he wrote stories for magazines far from the Ohio prison walls.

Most of his best friends and editorial associates in North Carolina and New York were unaware of the young man's incarceration or the conditions under which he was writing. It was only after his death that the truth finally came out: William Sydney Porter, who used the pen name O. Henry, had been imprisoned for three years for the charge of embezzling money from the Austin bank. Although scholars and biographers still disagree as to whether he committed the crime, O. Henry himself once referred to the prison sentence as a point in time at which he "fell heir to enough spare time to take up fiction writing seriously."

Some people shine under difficult circumstances. During his incarceration the author refined his writing and became known as the literary genius from whose pen flowed more than 200 stories, including such classics as "The Gift of the Magi" and "The Ransom of Red Chief."

Rather than bearing a grudge against the man for his alleged crime, Austin celebrates his literary achievements: His home on Fifth Street has been made into a museum. The O. Henry Museum hosts two main events annually honoring this man of letters: a birthday celebration on September 11 and the Pun-Off, because he was known for his plays on words.

Incidentally, in case you ever wondered where Porter got his pen name: It belonged to a prison guard by the name of Orrin Henry.

The Law West of the Pecos

Judge Roy Bean was the flamboyant, bigger-than-life judge who lived in southwest Texas in the 1880s. He was the epitome of the Texas mystique—that Texas was a place where you made your own laws, your own history, and even your own town.

Born in Kentucky around 1825, Roy left home at the age of 15 with his two brothers, Sam and Joshua. He had a trading post for a time in Chihuahua, Mexico, until he got in trouble with the law for killing a local, whereupon he lit out, as they say, for San Diego, where brother Joshua had become the town's first mayor. Joshua Bean appointed Roy a lieutenant in the state militia and made him a bartender in his bar called the Headquarters. Roy couldn't seem to stay out of trouble—his braggadocio and his penchant for gambling and cockfighting were always leading him to incite fights. It was once again time to leave when brother Joshua was killed by a jealous man in a fight over a woman, and this time Roy went to New Mexico, where his other brother, Sam, was sheriff.

Like Joshua, Sam also had a saloon. During the Civil War, when Roy wasn't tending bar, he was smuggling guns past the Union blockades. Moving to San Antonio in the 1870s, he married a young Mexican woman and with her had five children; the area where he lived is nicknamed Beanville. In 1882, with the railroads booming and laying track across Texas, Bean followed the boom, leaving his wife and children, and settled in Pecos County, where the commissioners there made him a Justice of the Peace.

The Jersey Lily Saloon in Langtry, Texas. Courtesy TexasEscapes.com.

Bean had a romantic streak, despite his flamboyant and aggressive ways: He was in love, or fancied himself in love, with a woman he'd never met. English actress Lillie Langtry had stolen his heart, and when the town of Langtry sprang up from the convergence of three railroads (where Bean made his home), it is said that the name came from his never-to-be-realized infatuation. Bean named his saloon there the Jersey Lily, after the actress's nickname, and from this spot, he dispensed jokes, drinks, and local law.

Although he has often been referred to as "the Hanging Judge," there is no actual proof that Bean ever hung anyone. One legend says that during his reign as "the law west of the Pecos," his saloon/courtroom was overseen by a pet bear. But he was even more flamboyant than that.

The year was 1898. At that time, prizefighting was illegal in many U.S. states and Mexico, but it was time for the championship battle between two famous boxers of the time, Peter Maher and Bob Fitzsimmons. February 22 of that year found more than 200 fans packing the Jersey Lily; after a drink (or two or three), Bean led the fans, along with the contestants, over a bridge to a sandbar on the Rio Grande. Because this was not in Mexico or the

United States, other lawmen, including a few Texas Rangers, could only watch in dismay as Bean held the prizefight, to the delight of the fans.

After Fitzsimmons knocked out Maher, Bean became a legend. A slew of movies have been made about his life, as have plenty of books. His story is also retold in the town of Langtry itself, where there is a fascinating Judge Roy Bean Visitor Center, complete with saloon, courtroom, and opera house as it might have looked when Bean held sway.

As for Bean himself, he now lies buried, along with his son, on the grounds of Whitehead Memorial Museum in Del Rio, in Big Bend Country.

Q & A

Q. What teacher and author wrote I'll Gather My Geese as a memoir of her life teaching and ranching in Big Bend Country?

Dr. Sophie Herzog, whom the people of Brazoria referred to as "Dr. Sophie." Courtesy of Texas State Library and Archives Commission.

A. The late Hallie Stillwell. She left behind a collection of antiques, mementos, and other paraphernalia related to life in this rugged land in Hallie's Hall of Fame Museum, just north of Big Bend National Park.

Q. What Austrian-born woman, trained as a physician, became known to railroad workers in the Brazoria area as "Dr. Sofie"?

A. Sofie Herzog, the first female railroad doctor in Texas. Not only did she care for the railroad workers' ills but she also removed so many bullets from wounded gunfighters that she had the bullets made into a necklace she wore for good luck. Her life is depicted in exhibits at the Brazoria Museum.

Q. What wildlife enthusiast and author, born in Gainesville in 1884, captured the imagination of international audiences with his tales of animal encounters long before Steve Irwin and Jane Goodall and was known for saying, "Bring 'em back alive"?

A. Frank Buck. He died in 1950, but the Frank Buck Zoo in Gainesville honors his memory and achievements.

BLACK GOLD AND COWBOY AND RODEO TALES

Spindletop and the Gladys City Boomtown

Back in the late 1800s, Beaumont was a sleepy little town near the coast, just east of the Louisiana border. Then a man named Patillo Higgins noticed oil coming up through the ground in the place called Spindletop Hill. A Sunday school teacher, Higgins took note of this when taking his students on picnics in the area. He must have been fascinated with this phenomenon, called oil seep, especially when it would sometimes erupt in flames (called gas flares).

Higgins asked three other men in town (J.F. Lamar, George W. Carroll, and George W. O'Brien) to go in with him on a little oil exploration venture. They agreed, and the Gladys City Oil, Gas, and Manufacturing Company was born.

The Lucas Gusher. Courtesy Spindletop Museum.

Their attempts at drilling oil were fruitless; they ran into dry well after dry well. Desperate, Higgins found a new partner in Austrian mining engineer Anthony F. Lucas. The engineer believed that underneath the salt domes, so populous in the area, were oil wells, with the "black gold" waiting to be tapped and brought to the surface. He asked two men from Pittsburgh, Pennsylvania to help finance a new oil well operation.

They agreed, and on January 10, 1901, that well blew in at 10:00 am. The gusher shot up approximately 100 feet in the air and flowed nine days before drillers Al and Curt Hamill could cap the well.

The world's first oil boomtown was born that day, and a new symbol was created that, along with the state flag and the Alamo, stands for Texas: the oil well. Today you can go visit a replica of what the city looked like back then. It's called Spindletop–Gladys City Boomtown and has a monument dedicated to the founder of the world's first oil well, Anthony F. Lucas.

Also in Beaumont, you van visit the Texas Energy Museum and learn more about oil exploration, production, and the refining process.

"The Roaring Ranger" Story

Eastland County was the site of great excitement in the early 1900s, for it was here that black gold was discovered, and the city of Ranger led the way of the oil boom. So named because of its proximity to a Texas Ranger camp, the town of Ranger earned national interest in October 1917, when its famous gusher, McClesky Number 1, began producing an unheard-of 1,700 barrels of oil a day (later, gushers produced upward of 11,000 barrels daily). Suddenly the sleepy town exploded into an active, chaotic place, with its population swelling from its original 1,000 to more than 30,000 in one year alone. Humble farmers became wealthy beyond their wildest dreams, railroad companies raced to be the first to construct infrastructure to the town, and when trains could get there, people with the "black gold flu" rode them, packing into the cars or even riding on top.

Because of all the drilling and commotion, the streets of the small town became muddy, with men in waders and hip boots carrying people on their backs across the streets for a fee. With the lure of easy money, vice too visited Ranger—in one day alone, there were five murders, and gambling and prostitution were common.

Despite all this, the town of Ranger did settle down, and in one year during its oil heyday, it made more people wealthy and in a bigger way than the gold fields of Alaska and California did—combined.

Today you can visit the much more sedate and charming city of Ranger. It has a junior college, a lake, some parks, and has the Roaring Ranger Museum. The museum, which is housed in what used to be the train station, is on Main Street and is open seven days a week.

DID YOU KNOW?

Gushing Gladewater

The city of Gladewater celebrates Texas's oil heritage with its annual East Texas Gusher Days, held every April. In Henderson—the site of the East Texas oil boom—is the Discovery Well you can visit even today. At its height of production, the Daisy Bradford Number 3 produced 300 barrels of oil per day.

Abilene, Abilene, Oiliest Town I've Ever Seen

You might have been singing the song this way if you'd been part of the 1981 centennial celebration. It seems that the city had established an exhibit to show how rigs drilled for oil—and accidentally struck black gold in the process!

Oil Movie

The 1941 movie about the oil-boom days of Texas, Boomtown, starring Spencer Tracy and Clark Gable, was filmed in Burkburnett, Texas.

Mamas, Don't Let Your Babies Grow Up to Be Cowgirls

The National Cowgirl Museum and Hall of Fame in Fort Worth is the only museum of its kind in the world, dedicating to honoring the achievements of women of the West. Some of the women highlighted include names that might surprise you, such as Willa Cather (who apparently did more than write), Georgia O'Keefe (the artist), Dale Evans, Annie Oakley, Patsy Cline, and Sacajawea, the guide for the Lewis and Clark Corps of Discovery.

All About the World's First Rodeo

The art and sport behind today's rodeo evolved from the daily skills employed by cowboys—saddling and breaking wild horses, trailing cattle, and roping and branding. In 1883 the town of Pecos made this into a competitive sport and became the site of the world's first rodeo.

Now, across the West (and elsewhere in the United States), rodeo competitions are everywhere. Rodeos sanctioned by the Professional Rodeo Cowboys Association include seven events for men such as calf roping, bull riding, and steer wrestling, and the women's event is barrel racing. Professional rodeo competitors have as their goal being able to get to the coveted destination of the rodeo circuit competition in Las Vegas every December—the National Finals Rodeo.

Back in Pecos, though, they haven't forgotten their roots. They celebrate their heritage with a nineteenth-century-style competition they call West of the Pecos every Fourth of July weekend. Also, at U.S. Highway 285 and First Street you will find the West of the Pecos Museum, which has taken up residence in an historic old hotel. The museum has loads of memorabilia related to the glory days of Pecos at the turn of the nineteenth century.

If you can't get to Pecos, there are more towns in

Texas celebrating rodeos than you can throw your lasso at, such as Stamford, which is the site of the "greatest amateur rodeo in the world."

. . . But the Cowboy Was Born Here

The charros of San Antonio share a revered history. Mexican rodeos are a time-honored tradition, especially in San Antonio. Photos this page courtesy Becky Crouch Patterson/2008 San Antonio Charro Association.

The town of Pecos might be the place where rodeo got its start, but in the South Texas Plains, Pleasanton's claim to fame is that it's the "Birthplace of the Cowboy." In its early days, it was located along the famous Chisholm Trail, where cowboys drove their herds to market (and local Jack Keller says that Pleasanton's first line of defense against Indian raids were the Longhorn steers!).

Much of the town still resembles postcards from

some Old West scene, so it comes by its moniker honestly. Not too long ago, they held an art competition based on the nickname "Birthplace of the Cowboy," coined by a local (Dr. Ben Parker). They came up with a drawing, used that on all their official town documents, and now celebrate the cowboy with an annual Cowboy Homecoming Days every fall, which they swear is the hottest celebration in the Lone Star State.

One Bodacious Tale

There are about 70 stock contractors who are members of the Professional Rodeo Cowboys Association; they produce or provide animals for more than 700 rodeos per year. They live on ranches, develop stock for competitions, and are the ultimate authority at any rodeo. Sammy Andrews of Addielou is one of these people—and in Texas and any other place that knows rodeo history, he and his bull, Bodacious, are synonymous with the sport.

Bodacious lies buried on the property of Sammy Andrews's ranch in this tiny town just east of Paris, near the Oklahoma border. Now lying underneath a rodeo chute as a tombstone, Bodacious was once both known and feared as "the world's most dangerous bull."

This was far from simply a dangerous bull—his reputation, even after his death in May 2000, is still vivid in the minds of rodeo-circuit riders, judges, and stockmen. Bodacious was inducted into the 1999 Pro Rodeo Hall of Fame in Colorado Springs, and owner Sammy Andrews retired the bull from the rodeo circuit before he got around to killing anyone who tried to ride him (out of 135 attempts, only six riders managed to stay on Bodacious the required eight seconds).

I caught up with Sammy Andrews, owner of the ranch, one hot June afternoon. "You mention the name

Bodacious to anyone in just about any part of the U.S.," he said, "and they'll know who you're talking about." Andrews said that because Bodacious had been such a superstar of the rodeo circuit, anyone who could manage to stay on became a superstar too.

This 1,800-pound bovine superstar was three times named the Professional Rodeo Cowboys Association bucking bull of the year—but what killed him was not trying to bust cowboys. He died of kidney failure. Bodacious was 12 years old.

Bodacious, the World's Most Dangerous Bull. Photo courtesy Sammy Andrews, Addielou, Texas.

"Anybody can come out and see where we've got him buried," Sammy said. Bodacious's legacy lives on in lots of stock, but the most famous one now is his son, who goes by the name of Bo's Excuse, according to Sammy. You can see Bo's Excuse walking the grounds of the ranch today. Bo's Excuse has been featured in Sports Illustrated, among other publications, but his famous sire was featured in GQ and even Playboy.

In 2004, the Houston Livestock Show and Rodeo honored Sammy Andrews, giving him a bucking chute to use as a memorial for Bodacious's grave. Sammy said that this was a chute Bodacious had bucked his giant way out of during rodeo competitions at the Houston Astrodome, so even the tombstone has a tie to the bull lying beneath. "There's no charge to come see Bodacious's grave," Sammy told me. "Everybody's welcome."

Stop in, if you're in the Paris area, and pay your respects—no bull.

So You Want to Live Like a Cowboy?

Even if you're a greenhorn, you can still like the life of a cowboy, even if only temporarily. Just like they did in the movie City Slickers, there are ranches catering to people who want to live their cowboy dream and saddle up for a day or even a week or two.

Throughout the state you'll find working cattle ranches of all kinds (such as the Wagon Wheel Ranch in Snyder). At these, you can work alongside real cowboys, herd cattle, and even eat on the trail, chuck wagon style. Most of these places I checked out require that you call "a-head" (sorry, I couldn't resist the pun).

Cowboys Writing Poetry? You Betcha!

The city of Alpine (in Big Bend Country) has as one of its annual events the Texas Cowboy Poetry Gathering every February. Chamber of Commerce staff member Andrew Suber told me that the requirements for the poetry competition aren't very stringent: "You don't have to be a cowboy, but the poetry often has the eternal themes of nature, fellowship, and the solitary life of a cowboy—although we do take a wider variety than only these topics," he said.

They encourage anyone who's written poetry to come out and see if they can take over the reins . . . er, mike.

If you can't make it to Alpine, Abilene (in the Panhandle) hosts the Western Heritage Classic every May, with part of the activities being a gathering of the Cowboy Poet's Society.

"Devil's Rope"—Yep, There's a Museum for That

The town of McLean (in the Panhandle region) has—believe it or not—a museum devoted to barbed wire. It shares the same building as the Route 66 Museum, so you can discover all you never knew about barbed wire, learn about the evolution of the cowboy, and see memorabilia devoted to old U.S. Highway 66, all in the same day.

The King of Barbed Wire

In the Old West, the indispensable tool for ranchers was barbed wire—it kept their cattle from roaming. Although this tool helped tame the Wild West (including Texas), it was a symbol of a loss of freedom for roaming cowboys and Native Americans and was a topic of many a heated debate in saloons, houses of worship, and parlors.

The "King of Barbed Wire" was Isaac Ellwood, who owned half of the patent for a type of barbed wire. Whichever side of the fence (pun intended) your ancestors were on in regard to the barbed-wire debates, they would all agree that he left behind a beautiful home in Port Arthur. Named Pompeiian Villa, it is listed on the National Register of Historic Places and is open for tours on weekdays.

Try to Win This Contest!

Northeast of Amarillo, the town of Miami (with a population of about 600) probably has a cow-to-person ratio of 5:1. Because this is the heart of ranching country, people naturally go out and call their cows to get fed on a daily basis.

Back in 1949, the people of Miami decided to have a regular competition for this talent and started their National Cow-Calling Contest. The contestants have to be loud, if not talented, and judges are positioned up to a mile away from the stage. The annual contest is held the first weekend in June and is said to be a "moo-ving" experience.

Mooving Along

If you want to see a cattle drive—on any given day—go to Plainview. It's here they have a herd of 45 colorful cows roaming the city. They're not real cows: These are made of fiberglass! They were originally created to help promote the city's Cowboy Days, celebrated every second Saturday in September.

If you can't get to Plainview, Bowie has the Chisholm Trail Memorial Park, which commemorates the cattle drives along this famous trail with a series of statues. In this park, a herd of nine life-size Longhorn steer, with two cowboys driving them, makes for a good photo opportunity.

Of course, if you want to see the real, breathing bovine—go to Fort Worth, where they have a cattle drive every day. The cattle are herded down Exchange Avenue twice a day.

A King Among Ranches

You can credit the city of Kingsville (with a population of roughly 26,000), just southwest of Corpus Christi, for being the birthplace of the ranching industry in America, for this is the location of the world-renowned King Ranch.

It all began when in 1853, when riverboat captain Richard King bought 75,000 acres of land here. It was part of a Spanish land grant known as Santa Gertrudis. King began breeding cattle, naming the unique strain after the land grant. The Santa Gertrudis breed is known today as the first strain of cattle that had its origins in the Western Hemisphere.

King didn't stop there. He was dissatisfied with the lackluster quality of leather products (especially saddles) that were commercially available and started his own saddle-making business. These he made available to his ranch workers, known as kinenos. Later, political leaders and foreign dignitaries, hearing of King's quality leather goods, purchased items from his shop as well.

From its humble beginnings in the 1800s to the booming cattle-and-saddle business it is today, King Ranch has maintained its original vision that's a reflection of what you would think defines Texas: be big, think big, and plan big. Today, King Ranch is bigger than the state of Rhode Island, consisting of 825,000 acres, with more than 60,000 cattle.

When you go to Kingsville, there is plenty to see and do there, mostly relating to King Ranch. The sprawling ranch itself is open for tours, you can visit the King Ranch Museum, the King Ranch Saddle Shop, and several other parks and museums in the city.

Cowboy Up . . . But Behind Bars

It was in 1931 and times were hard in Texas, just as they were everywhere else in the country. The prison system was affected by the Great Depression, and something had to be done to raise money to maintain it. Lee Simmons, general manager of the Texas prison system, came up with the idea of having the inmates host a rodeo, and not just host it, but be the cowboys in the competition. The Texas Prison Rodeo was born.

Albert Moore, prison welfare director, headed up the new organization and planned the early rodeos with help from Walter Waid (then warden) and R.O. McFarland, livestock supervisor. At first, only a handful of locals, inmates, and prison employees came to watch the rodeo competitors as they tried their mettle against their hooved antagonists, and for lack of a better space in which to hold it, the first few rodeos were held in the prison's baseball stadium.

The rodeo was a hit; Simmons knew that he had latched onto a good idea. In a few years, the crowds swelled to more than 15,000, and the Sunday event came to be the largest sporting event in the state, in terms of attendees. In some years, fans numbered more than 100,000.

Only one year was the rodeo not held—in 1943, because of World War II. When it opened in 1944 as a victory rodeo, proceeds from it were invested in the war effort. Growing in popularity, the show went on the road in 1950, to Dallas. The baseball stadium was replaced by a new, modern structure, and weekday performances were added to accommodate the crowds.

Other entertainment was added, with such notables as Johnny Cash, Dolly Parton, Curly Fox, Eddie Arnold, Ernest Tubb, Johnny Rodriguez, George Strait, and Tom T. Hall performing. It seemed to be something that would go on forever.

In 1986, however, because of funding conflicts, the last chute was closed with the final rodeo performance of October 26. The mother–daughter duo of the Judds, Naomi and Wynonna, entertained the crowds as the last singing act of the rodeo. Some people hope that the Texas Prison Rodeo will one day return, but for now, it is only a memory in the minds of those who were there . . . on both sides of the bars.

Q & A

Q. In the city of Iraan, what is the name of the oil well there that is still one of the largest oil-producing wells in the country?

A. Discovery Well A Number 1

Q. What university became one of the richest schools in the United States when its Santa Rita No. 1 struck oil in Big Lake, Texas?

A. The University of Texas

Q. Who and where is the nation's largest cowboy?

A. Big Tex towers over the Texas State Fairgrounds at a height of 52 feet. He's the official mascot of the State Fair of Texas, held every year in Dallas.

Q. What three towns used to have the nickname Six Shooter Junction and why?

A. Harlingen, because Texas Rangers and townspeople would gather in a particular spot in town for target practice; Hempstead, because there was so much violence there around the turn of the eighteenth century (the most violent event to come from that area in Hempstead occurred in 1905, when U.S. Congressman John Pinckney, his brother, and two other men were gunned down inside the courthouse); and Waco, because of its general frontier wildness

Q. What town is known as Cowboy Capital of the World?

A. Bandera, which has more rodeos, as well as more working and dude ranches within its borders, than any other town

Q. The infamous Mason County War, also known as the Hoodoo War, was between German settlers and native Texans. What sparked this bloody conflagration?

A. Cattle thieving

Q. In what town will you find the Branding Wall, with at least 230 cattle brands that reveal the importance of ranching to this area and to Texas?

A. The Branding Wall is located in Colorado City, in Kiwanis Park.

Q. What was the name of what used to be the world's largest ranch?

A. The XIT Ranch, the world's largest in the 1880s, covered more than 3 million acres. It has since been parceled off to smaller ranches.

Q. Where in Fort Worth can you see the Last Great Gunfight of the Old West (a reenactment) every February, as well as the Texas Trail of Fame, which has bronze-inlaid markers along the walkway commemorating individuals significant to the Western/cowboy way of life?

A. In the Stockyards National Historic District

Q. What town honors the contributions of the leather industry to the West with the Land of Leather Days Festival, held every February?

A. Yoakum

RELIGION AND UTOPIAN COMMUNITIES

A Utopia in Dallas

When you go to Dallas, you may pass by Reunion Arena, which actually has nothing to do with a reunion per se. The Reunion Arena and nearby Reunion Tower are both named for a utopian community that once existed about three miles away.

Formed in 1855 by Swiss, French, and Belgian settlers, the community of La Reunion was established as a socialist utopia, one of more than 40 similar colonies throughout America during the nineteenth century. It was founded on the philosophies of François Marie Charles Fourier, who suggested a specific approach to a communal lifestyle that included women's voices in the democratic process.

The settlers who came to the area might have succeeded except for two things: the lack of a talent for farming and the influence of Mother Nature. Although many of the colonists were talented in such trades as tailoring, shoemaking, watchmaking, and such (some were even good brewmasters), they lacked sufficient knowledge of farming to make their colony thrive. That, combined with a disastrous blizzard (which struck in May 1856, a one-of-a-kind phenomenon that had never happened before and never has since), followed by summer plagued with grasshoppers and drought, saw most of the colonists either returning to their homelands or moving into the growing city of Dallas.

Some might think that this effort to create an ideal-istic city was a failure, but it wasn't a total loss: Dallas ben-efited greatly from this influx of talented craftsmen into its area. The city that, given its newness, should have been raw and unsophisticated suddenly became one of the jew-els of Texas, a dynamic regional market enriched by the cultural diversity of its European newcomers. Because of La Reunion and her former inhabitants, Dallas had its first brewery, a butcher shop, and a carriage factory, as well as a great cultural basis in the form of poets, philosophers, botanists, and other members of the intelligentsia.

When you visit Dallas, you'll find a few reminders of La Reunion. On Fort Worth Avenue on Cockrell Hill, a few La Reunion colonists' graves still exist in the old Fish Trap Cemetery. North of downtown Dallas, there is a park named after famous La Reunion botanist Julien Rever-chon, who went on to become professor of botany at Bay-lor University College of Medicine and Pharmacy. There is also a street in Dallas named after another La Reunion botanist, Jacob Boll. Named in honor of the utopian com-munity, the Reunion Arena used to be home of the Dallas Mavericks basketball team and Dallas Stars hockey team and sits at the southwest corner of downtown Dallas; it is near the Hyatt Regency Dallas complex. The Reunion Tower, mentioned earlier, has at its top a sphere adorned with hundreds of lights that can be seen for miles—a re-minder of the light that can shine from just a few people.

The most bittersweet of these is the stone marker found at the back of the Stevens Park golf course tee box. It can be seen from Hampton Boulevard south of Fort Worth Avenue. It reads:

Site of the French colony
La reunion
Settled 1854.

Placed by Jane Douglas Chapter
Daughters of the
American Revolution
April 10, 1924.

La Reunion lives on, in its historical legacy and in the people who continue to remember it. For example, Gil R. Glover, a Dallas writer, was quoted in Dallas View as saying the La Reunion colonists helped create entirely new markets by enriching the Dallas economy. The Reunion colonists, he said, gave a "unique and priceless boost to a frontier city" in the early days of Texas.

When you visit Dallas, do go see the stone marker commemorating the establishment of this short-lived utopian community and remember the extensive European influence Dallas had in her early days, an influence that is still felt today.

DID YOU KNOW?

Godly Things

Looming above the city of El Paso, at the place where Texas, Mexico, and New Mexico meet, there is a 4,576-foot high summit called Sierra de Cristo Rey, which means "Mountain of Christ the King." Atop the mountain you can see a huge statue of Christ on the cross, carved from limestone quarried in Austin and created by sculptor Urbici Soler. The steep mountain is climbed during pilgrimages on the last Sunday in October.

In Ballinger is a 100-foot cross created by the Jim and Doris Studer family. It too is nothing small—it weighs 50 tons—and adjacent to it is a grotto and a statue of Our Lady of Guadelupe.

Utopian Boerne

The town of Boerne (pronounced BURN-ee), in the Hill Country, was founded in 1849 by German settlers aspiring to live out the ideals of philosopher Thomas More as he put forth his thoughts on the epitome of social organization in his Utopia writings. With a population of just about 9,000, it's still the ideal place for people who enjoy living in a cultured climate that still has the charm of small-town life.

The friendly people of Boerne continue to celebrate their German heritage too, so whenever you visit, you will be Wilkommen.

Ideal Living in Sugar Land

Originally named because it was headquarters to Imperial Sugar, the city of Sugar Land, in Fort Bend County, seems to be a modern-day utopia. Imperial Sugar's main refining and distribution center was located here and was so much a part of Sugar Land's history that the crown logo for Imperial Sugar remains a part of the city seal and logo.

The many recreational activities and programs that the town offers to its 76,000-plus residents also have caused it to receive the Fittest City in Texas award every year since 2004. Sugar Land continues to have an economic boom—according to U.S. Bureau of Census's 2005 statistics, Sugar Land is the fastest-growing city in the Lone Star state. It also has the largest number of master-planned communities in the nation. It's home to Western Airways and many other successful companies dealing in everything from software to engineering and energy production.

Architectural Delight: The Bishop's Palace

The Bishop's Palace at dusk in Galveston. Courtesy Diocese of Galveston.

A beautiful home in Galveston was built in 1886 and later purchased to be the home of the bishop of the Archdiocese of Galveston–Houston. It's not just beautiful: The home, known as the Bishop's Palace, is the only building in Texas listed among the American Institute of Architects' 100 outstanding buildings in the United States.

If the Venetian crystal chandelier or the elaborate staircase made of different exotic woods doesn't entice you to agree, then check out the bedrooms, the beautiful wall covering imported from England, or the mantel that won first place at the 1876 World's Fair in Philadelphia. The Bishop's Palace is open seven days a week for tours and oohs and aahs. It is managed by the Galveston Historical Foundation and owned by the Catholic Diocese of Galveston.

Orange You Glad They Came Here?

In 1824, some Oblate Fathers (Roman Catholic monks) established a mission in Mission, Texas. One thing they grew there, as an agricultural experiment, was oranges. The orange grove grew and began to thrive, and now the town has too. John Shary, who is now known as the father of the Texas citrus industry, was the first to grow the fruit as a commercial venture. Now, every January, the town holds its Texas Citrus Fiesta.

Catholic Landholders

Sam Houston was baptized as a Catholic at the Sterne-Hoya Home in Nacogdoches, because at that time Mexico required its landholders to be of that faith.

The home is now a historic site, open to the public for tours.

A Spiritual Utopia: The Eckankar Religion

A faith that refers to itself as the "religion of the light and sound of God," Eckankar, headquartered in Texas, is growing in the face of so much disillusionment with traditional religions. With members throughout the state and in more than 100 countries, the religion has as its cornerstone the belief that there is, in the words of its Web site, "an audible life current." This life current, they say, is known as the ECK, or Holy Spirit.

The religion stresses spiritual exercises that will enable seekers to tap into the life current and gain increased divine understanding. When I contacted Eckankar member Don Elefante for more information, he wrote that there were active groups in Dallas, Fort Worth, Austin, San Antonio, and Houston, and other smaller groups in El Paso and the Rio Grande Valley.

Members of the Eckankar religion have meetings and classes, and although these are open to members only, other activities are open to the public, such as worship services, book discussion classes, and informational events, to let more people know about the scope and focus of this unique faith. There is also an annual regional seminar for the purpose of putting the word out to other spiritual seekers.

Check out their Web site (see the "Virtual Texas" section near the back of this book). And happy seeking.

The Utopia That Went Awry

It began with a sect that split from the Seventh-Day Adventist Church, and once members had a common goal and vision: to share in the glory on the day of the Apocalypse, when Jesus would return to Earth and the world as we know it would end.

Various leaders of the church under founder Ellen White had prophesied different dates as to when this would happen, and again and again followers had gathered in anticipation of the day, only to be repeatedly disillusioned when it didn't happen. In 1930, a group of these disillusioned members left the church. They were led by a man named Victor Houteff. He moved his followers to Tyler, Texas, and began once again preparing for Jesus' Second Coming. He named his group the Davidians, after the biblical King David.

Jesus didn't make his reappearance on the date set by Houteff either. When Houteff later died, his widow Florence took up the Second Coming prophecy torch and announced Jesus would return on Easter Sunday of 1959. When this too proved false, a member of the congregation named Benjamin Roden established his own branch of the church, and called it the Branch Davidians.

When Roden passed away, while his widow Lois took up where he'd left off, a high school dropout appeared on the scene. Named Vernon Wayne Howell, he had taught himself scripture and believed he was one of God's chosen. The teen had been thrown out of the Seventh-Day Adventist Church of Tyler for being disrespectful toward church leaders, for his shabby appearance, and for his negative attitude. After his banishment in 1981, he left Waco, discovered the Branch Davidian sect in Tyler, and began preaching to them.

Telling the members he was the seventh angel mentioned in the Book of Revelation (the angel of the seventh star, Revelations chapter 11 and also chapter 3, verse 14), Howell captured the imagination of the sect. (By way of explanation, see Revelation 22:16: "I, Jesus, have sent my angel to testify to you these things in the Churches. I am The Root and The Off-Spring of David, The Bright and Morning Star.")

The Branch Davidians embraced him as one of their own, and Lois Roden proclaimed Howell as her successor when it came time for her to depart this life. She also encouraged members who had abandoned the group to return and listen to the young man who, apparently, was bestowed with charisma. A year later, in 1984, Howell married Rachel Jones, who was daughter of Lois Roden's close associate, Perry Jones, probably as a way of cementing his hold on the group.

This claim to succession did not go unchallenged: Lois Roden's son George disputed Howell's hold, saying he, not Howell, should be the new leader. He went so far as to hold an election, which he won, then changed the name of the settlement from Mount Carmel to Rodenville.

Howell left, accompanied by his wife and a handful of followers, and resettled in East Texas (Palestine), where the group lived a barely sustainable existence in wooden shacks, with little food and no plumbing or heat. Undeterred, the young visionary gave sermons and had his group study scripture. Then he took an unthinkable step.

Howell began claiming other male members' wives, sweethearts, and daughters as his property—as with all else on the settlement grounds. Amazingly, the group did not question this. He then took his preaching to the road and gathered a diverse group of followers from all over the country and even as far away as Australia to join him at the spare settlement in East Texas, where they would live until they could retake the original settlement in Mount Carmel.

In late 1987, Howell and his followers managed to retake Mount Carmel by convoluted legal means and moved from Palestine to Mount Carmel in Waco. Like his apocalyptic predecessors, he began preaching that Armageddon would happen soon, and in 1990, he changed his name to David Koresh, after the biblical King David (the name Koresh came from the Hebrew name for the famous Persian ruler, Cyrus).

Koresh ordered his followers to tear down all of the old buildings in the compound, and Mount Carmel was transformed into something looking more like a military facility expecting an imminent siege. The centerpiece of this facility was a three-story watchtower, where followers could monitor traffic coming from all directions. The followers also dug tunnels in preparation for air attack and began to practice target shooting.

Meanwhile, Koresh continued to claim other male followers' women and daughters as his own; many of the children born during this time were of his lineage. Koresh went even further and separated the men's, women's, and children's sleeping quarters.

For some of the followers, particularly a few from Australia, all of this was simply too much. They reported these bizarre activities to the local district attorney and sheriff. When Koresh heard of these complaints, he told his people to prepare themselves for an outside attack and changed the name of the compound to Ranch Apocalypse.

Tensions began to rise when in 1992, a delivery driver inadvertently broke open a package slated to be dropped off at Koresh's ranch. It contained hand grenades; this was reported first to the sheriff's office, then to the U.S. Bureau of Alcohol, Tobacco and Firearms (ATF).

This evidence was sufficient for authorities to act: ATF agents began to follow all items scheduled to be delivered to Ranch Apocalypse, and they discovered thousands of pounds in weapons (such as grenade launchers and M-16 rifles) and ammunition that could be traced to the Branch Davidians. To more closely monitor ranch activities, the agents leased a house nearby and one of the ATF agents infiltrated the cult, acting as a new recruit.

With increasing pressure—especially from the media—about the weapons, Koresh's bizarre extramarital relationships, and later rumors of child abuse, the ATF decided to stage a raid on Ranch Apocalypse. On February 28, 1993, hundreds of armed agents boarded vehicles and headed for the ranch. The undercover ATF agent overheard a Davidian telling Koresh about the imminent raid and sent word to his ATF contacts that this raid was not going to be a surprise.

The undercover agent was right: Koresh and his followers were ready for the raid, and after a two-hour exchange of bullets in which four ATF agents and several Branch Davidians lost their lives (with more wounded), media from television and newspapers swarmed into Waco to cover the story. The standoff continued into March, and the FBI came to assist the ATF. Meanwhile, prior to this, Koresh had released followers wanting to leave the compound on the condition that he be allowed to broadcast personal messages using a local radio station.

The Branch Davidians began to be inundated with noise and lights during all hours, because the ATF was trying to deprive them of sleep. All shipments of food and other supplies were stopped from entering the compound.

Finally, the FBI decided to stop allowing more followers to leave Ranch Apocalypse (probably reasoning that these would pressure Koresh to give himself up); the last person left March 24, 1993. There were just under 100 followers left inside.

The standoff continued into April, when Koresh announced he was going to write his own interpretation of the Book of Revelation, and when he was finished, he would turn himself in. When this too didn't happen, it was decided to force the followers and Koresh out of the compound using tear gas.

Agents attacked the compound with cranes and tanks, which knocked holes in the walls, and shot canisters of tear gas inside. For reasons that are still unclear, however, the compound caught on fire, and 78 Branch Davidians, including Koresh, died in the blaze. Eleven people escaped, but the other men, women, and children inside died.

The newly appointed attorney general (under President Bill Clinton), Janet Reno, publicly assumed responsibility for the attacks. At the end of that year, 1993, the remaining Branch Davidians were brought to trial, and the U.S. government charged them with conspiracy and killing the ATF agents (they were found guilty of possessing illegal weapons); their sentences ranged from 5 to 40 years. These sentences were reimposed in 1997 by Judge Walter Smith after a review of the case.

This incident has been criticized as time has gone by. Many people claim that the government should not have charged the compound, causing everything to come to a head as it did. It has also been pointed out that the huge amount of media attention Koresh's group received added the proverbial fuel to the fire.

Today, the Branch Davidian movement continues, but it is in two groups: an anti-Koresh group and one composed of his faithful few. A museum has been put on the site to commemorate the tragedy. The followers of Koresh have prophesied his return (which didn't happen as announced) and have made other, similar proclamations, none of which have materialized. Koresh's followers are still waiting for him to return and take them to the Promised Land.

The tragedy of Ranch Apocalypse continues to have far-reaching effects. Relatives of the dead and those surviving the tragedy have an ongoing lawsuit against the federal government, saying that agents started the blaze and are responsible for the deaths of all of the people inside. In 1999, the U.S. Department of Justice continued to maintain that the FBI and the ATF did not use any pyrotechnic devices and could not have been to blame for the deaths. In 2000, U.S. District Judge Walter Smith cleared the federal government of intentional wrongdoing in the deaths of the Branch Davidians, saying the one person entirely to blame for the deaths was David Koresh. An advisory jury reached the same conclusion that year.

Many books and magazine articles have been written about the tragedy. Views of various and sundry "experts" range from condemnation of the government to placing the total blame on Koresh. The most horrible tragedy may be the group's journey from a visionary religion to a destructive, doomsday cult that ultimately doomed itself.

Mission Country, USA

Did you know that many missions in Texas are older than most others in the United States—including California? Here is just a sample of some missions you can explore in the Lone Star State:

El Paso

In El Paso, you'll find San Elizario Presidio Chapel, founded in 1777; Nuestra Señora de la Concepcion del Socorro, founded in 1682; and Nuestra Señora del Carmen, established in 1681. The latter is the oldest mission in the state.

San Antonio

Mission Nuestra Señora de la Purísima Concepción was founded in 1731 and is the oldest unrestored stone church in the United States. Mission San Francisco de la Espada was also established in 1731 but has been restored. Mission San José y San Miguel de Aguayo is also known as "Queen of Missions" and was founded in 1720. The Mission San Juan Capistrano was also established in 1731, like the first two, and continues to serve a congregation.

Groom, Texas: Spiritual Mecca?

If you travel due east of Amarillo, you'll see two things in the tiny town of Groom (with a population just under 600 as of press time) that might cause you to pause for introspection. One is Blessed Mary's Restaurant, where you can have a good meal, and then whatever you pay into the jug by the door goes to charity. Their specialty is beef enchiladas.

The other is on the southern side of Interstate 40.

The cross in Groom, Texas. Note how small the windmills at the base appear. Courtesy Einar Einarsson Kvaran.

Known as the Cross of Our Lord Jesus Christ, the steel structure, created by engineer Steve Thomas (with the help of his wife Bobby), is currently the second-largest cross in the entire Western Hemisphere. It stands 190 feet tall and is lit up at night.

This is not just any cross either. It was put together in two welding shops in nearby Pampa, with more than 100 welders lending their expertise. To put it up in Groom required every concrete truck to be had from the nearby counties to pour the foundation, but the herculean job was successfully completed in July 1995.

Take note of the photo accompanying this story and you can see the windmills at the feet of the cross, dwarfed by its size. If you visit Groom, you can also tour the Stations of the Cross and gift shop adjacent to the cross Thomas created. More than 10 million people now stop by the cross annually, and thousands have mailed the Thomases their messages of thanks and praise since then (see "Virtual Texas" near the back of this book for the Web site address).

Today's Sermon, by George!

George Foreman, famed boxing legend and creator of the "Lean, Mean, Grilling Machine," is now a preacher. He found God after losing a boxing match in 1977 to Jimmy Young. Now, he can be found at the preacher's podium at Houston's Church of the Lord Jesus Christ on any given Sunday.

I'll bet nobody goes to sleep when he's preaching.

Q & A

Q. What town is one of the oldest Polish communities, and thus one of the oldest Polish parishes, in the United States?

A. The town of Bandera

Q. How do the Franciscan Poor Clare Nuns at the monastery in Brenham support themselves?

A. They raise miniature horses. You can visit their horse farm and gift shop most days.

Q. What city was established initially as a "sobriety settlement" by Methodist minister L.H. Carhart?

A. Clarendon

Q. What ideal community was established in Wharton County by Danish settlers and was named "the Danish capital of Texas" in 1991 by the state legislature?

A. Danevang, which still has a strong Danish community today

Q. When the people of Danevang lost their church in a hurricane in 1945, in what unique way did they replace it?

A. By buying the chapel building from Camp Hulen, a deactivated army training base located in Palacios

Q. What old-time judge is remembered in history as a preserver of old-time religion?

A. Thomas Whitfield Davidson

Q. What man held the first meeting of Methodists in Texas, and where?

A. Samuel Doak McMahon, who held the meeting just outside San Augustine in 1832

Q. What famous Methodist preacher helped Francis A. Wilson and Daniel Poe establish Wesleyan College in San Augustine?

A. Littleton Fowler; he came from Tennessee to Texas in 1837 on a mission trip—and stayed

Q. What city is the site of the first Roman Catholic convent in Texas?

A. Galveston. St. Mary Cathedral, the oldest Catholic cathedral in the state, is also there.

Q. What church in Galveston never missed a service—even during hurricane season?

A. Trinity Episcopal Church. It was always repaired immediately after any hurricane damage and has never missed holding a service since its completion in 1848.

Q. Padre Island was given its name to honor an early settler who was a Catholic priest. What was his name?

A. Padre Jose Nicolas Balli

Q. What was the original religion of the Society of the Burning Bush, which had an ideal community called the Metropolitan Institute of Texas (eastern Texas) in the early 1900s?

A. They were originally Methodists. The community dissolved because of agricultural problems in the 1920s.

Q. What shrine is in Sabine Pass and was dedicated by Our Lady of Guadalupe Catholic Church in 2002?

A. A 17-foot-tall bronze statue of Our Lady of Guadalupe is there, set on rocks brought from Mount Tepeyac, where the Virgin Mary is said to have appeared to peasant Juan Diego.

Q. What town has a prayer tower, complete with bells from France, and a chapel for prayer—open 24 hours a day?

A. Pittsburg, Texas. It is located in Witness Park, at the intersection of Lafayette and Jefferson streets.

SPORTS STORIES

The Dallas Cowboys: Hearts as Big as Texas

Unless you've been in a coma, you probably know the impact the Dallas Cowboys have made on the National Football League since the team's inception in 1959. What you may not know, however, is that these players are about as true a team as any you'd find in the country.

Case in point: In training camp the summer prior to the 1981 football season, athletes Ron Springs and Everson Walls became fast friends. In the years they played together (1981 through 1984), they remained close, as did their kids.

Springs had diabetes, though, and suffered complications from the debilitating disease, losing his right foot and some left toes in the process. Problems with his kidneys caused his hands to swell and curl into useless fists. Walking was out of the question. His diabetes was becoming life-threatening when Walls came to his aid. Learning that Springs needed a kidney transplant and that relatives who had offered to donate had been deemed unacceptable matches by Springs's physicians, Walls offered Springs one of his own kidneys.

The transplant operation happened in March 2007, and now expectations are high that Springs will be able to walk on his own. According to CBS's Sportsline.com, this is the first time in sports history that two former professional athletes from the same team have taken part in a transplant operation where one gave to the other.

That kind of devotion is, to me, what really makes a winning team.

And While You're At It, Bring On the Cheerleaders!

No one would deny that part of the attraction of the Dallas Cowboys is their cheerleaders, and with good cause: This team of highly trained athletes—part professional dancer, part ambassador, part model—is a facet of the image that makes the Dallas Cowboys so successful, with an ever-growing fan base.

Kelli Finglass, the director of the Dallas Cowboys Cheerleaders (DCC), was recently interviewed on a Country Music Television special featuring the DCC tryouts. A cheerleader herself since 1984, she offered this information to viewers:

- The minimum age for anyone trying out to become a DCC is 18. There is no upper age limit.
- Those trying out have to be high school graduates.
- In tryouts, the veteran cheerleaders—in other words, the current DCC—have to compete with the new competitors, so that no one becomes complacent.

The DCCs hold themselves up to, in Finglass's words, "uncompromised standards of excellence," and it shows in everything they do, on and off the field. Like the Dallas Cowboys—who, by the way, participate in philanthropic efforts of their own, such as working with the Salvation Army—the DCC are active in their communities, the country, and the world. Recently, for example, they traveled to Iraq to support and entertain the troops there as part of a USO tour. Jim Outenreath, a native of Garland, Texas, working in Iraq in September 2007 as a government contractor, posted this comment on the DCC Web site: "Seeing these talented and beautiful young ladies was an honor. . . . [They] put a smile on everyone's face."

Whether the smile shows up in Iraq or on the field, it's sure to be as big as Texas if it was inspired by the DCC.

If you want to see more of the Dallas Cowboys and their cheerleaders, there is a guided tour of Texas Stadium in Irving you can take—on every day except game day.

A Bowl of . . . History: Texas Tech

It was Friday night, December 29, 2006, and Texas Tech University's Red Raiders were down by 31 points at halftime in the Insight Bowl, playing against the University of Minnesota's Golden Gophers. Most teams and their coaches would have said, "It's over," but that wasn't what tenacious coach Mike Leach thought.

In the locker room in his halftime talk to his team, Leach told his players just what he thought about where they stood. He told his team that rather than give up, they had an opportunity to make history, and, according to his interview with the Associated Press, "play all 60 minutes."

Make history they did: in what the Associated Press called one of the "more improbable victories in its history," Texas Tech came out on the field for the second half of the game and emerged victorious, 44–41. As of press time, this remains the largest come-from-behind victory in Division I-A bowl history.

Interestingly, the previous bowl record was also made by a team from Texas: the Marshall Thundering Herd, which had scored 30 points against the East Carolina Pirates in the GMAC Bowl of 2001 and whose legendary victories inspired the 2006 movie We Are Marshall.

The Sports Matching Game

These sports heroes hail from Texas. Match the description with the sports star (answers below, but don't peek!).

1. Winner of the Tour de France seven times; a testicular cancer survivor, he has championed this cause.

2. Given the ironic nickname "Gentle _____" by fellow golfers because of his temper, he won the Masters Golf Tournament in 1995. Known as one of golf's greatest putters.

3. Nicknamed for a baseball star of her era and born Mildred Didrikson; adept in many athletic endeavors, she was considered by many as one of the greatest women athletes of all time. A museum in Beaumont commemorates her many achievements.

4. Born in Houston in 1935, he is popularly regarded as the greatest American race car driver in history. Holds the all-time United States Auto Club record with 159 racing victories; inducted into the International Motorsports Hall of Fame in 2000.

5. A well-known boxing champion, he has four children who all bear his first name, and sells his Lean Mean Grilling Machine on television.

6. Olympic gold medalist and gymnast popular for her charming, mile-wide smile. A resident of Houston, she won in the 1984 Olympic Games in Los Angeles the All-Around Gold Medal in women's gymnastics—the only all-around Olympic title ever given to an American.

7. Elected to the National Baseball Hall of Fame in 1999, this man was born in Refugio, Texas, and last played for the Texas Rangers. He holds the all-time record of 5,714 strikeouts.

8. Football star whose hometown is Tyler, Texas, and is nicknamed "the Tyler Rose;" won the Heisman Trophy in 1977. Has played with the Houston Oilers and the New Orleans Saints.

9. Born in 1949 in McKinney, he's a longtime friend of "Gentle _____." He won the U.S. Open in 1992, but his

first Professional Golfers' Association of America tour win came in 1976. He was elected to the World Golf Hall of Fame in 2004.

10. Born in Dallas in 1939 into poverty, this man pulled himself up from that life and discovered golf. He is the only golfer to the British Open, the U.S. Open, and the Canadian Open in the same year (1971).

a.   George Foreman
b.   Nolan Ryan
c.   Earl Campbell
d.   Lance Armstrong
e.   A.J. Foyt
f.   Lee Trevino
g.   Tom Kite
h.   Mary Lou Retton
i.   Babe Zaharias
j.   Ben Crenshaw

Answers: 1, d; 2, j; 3, i; 4, e; 5, a; 6, h; 7, b; 8, c; 9, g; 10, f.

Tom Landry, the Maker of "America's Team"

Born in Mission, Texas, in 1924, Landry went on to be a football player (defensive back) with the New York Giants. In 1960, he became coach of the Dallas Cowboys when they were a motley crew of misfits and made them into a team of truly professional football players. Known for his signature creation, the flex defense, he coached the Cowboys through 29 seasons, winning 18 division championships and bringing the team to five Super Bowls (they won two of those).

Mission remembers its native son with a mural of the coach who made the Cowboys "America's team." The mural shows aspects of his life and career, and in the sidewalk below the mural are impressions of Landry's hands and feet.

You Hunters Out There, Give These Guys a Hand (Literally)!

The town of Olney in north Texas is one of the greatest places in the state for hunting birds, white-tailed deer, turkey, and other game. It's also the place for a type of hunting you won't find anywhere else in the world.

In 1972, a couple of hunters (the former county commissioner and city manager) were discussing the upcoming dove season. These two hunters were challenged: They each had only one arm. In their discussion, they began talking about how other one-armed hunters might enjoy getting together for a dove hunt of their own.

That first year, 16 one-armed hunters came to the hunt. Now, the list has grown to more than 550 invitees!

DID YOU KNOW?

Making Major League History: Frank Robinson

Born in Beaumont in 1935, Frank Robinson was the first African American manager in baseball history, as well as the only player to have snagged an MVP (Most Valuable Player) award in each league. He was once quoted as saying he'd rather be known as simply the manager of the Cleveland Indians instead of the first black manager.

Young Driver

The youngest winner in the Grand-Am Rolex Sports Car Series at the Daytona International Speedway was Colin Braun, 17, from Ovalo, Texas. Braun won his history-making race in June 2006. Yay, Colin!

Hell (on Wheels) Week in Texas

Texas Hell Week, a week-long bicycling marathon phenomenon, started when some friends—one of whom had moved back to Texas from the Midwest—got together during spring break of 1991 to do some major biking. At first, their trek was on a smaller scale, originating from San Marcos. That first year, five friends joined the Texas transplant. The fourth year, the route—along Interstate 35—was getting too busy and the group had grown. Finally, they settled on Fredericksburg (about an hour due west of Austin) as the starting point; and the number of riders has swelled to nearly 400.

The success of Texas Hell Week—so called because the bikers ride nearly across the state—has caused such a buzz that the originators have a similar biking marathon in Florida (Gator Country Hell Week), California (Viva Las Vegas Hell Week), and Wisconsin (Cheese Country Hell Week).

Another Legend

In September 2006, University of Texas head track and field and cross-country coach Bev Kearney was honored at the 21st Annual Great Sports Legend Dinner. She was one of nine sport celebrities in the class of 2006, recognized for her contributions to the track and field competitions and to the coaching profession. She was joined at the dinner by other greats, such as Lance Armstrong and Tony Hawk.

Kearny has made track and field history with her work. As of press time, her accomplishments include leading the University of Texas Longhorns to six National Collegiate Athletic Association (NCAA) national championships, but there's more to her than just wanting to win: With a heart as big as Texas, Kearny has also served as mentor to 14 national champions who have collectively won 28 NCAA crowns.

This Story Will Give You Paws

Texas A&M University's team, the Aggies, has as its mascot a collie. The collie's name has always been Reveille, after the tune played during the Aggies' football games.

When four of the Reveilles were moved from their burial sites in 1997, fans were outraged, even though it was for a good cause—for the expansion of Kyle Field, the university's football stadium. One of the Aggie traditions says that the dogs must be buried facing the scoreboard inside its College Station stadium, and this was no longer possible.

The fans thought of a way to remedy this, though, and put up a small scoreboard near where the Reveilles were moved, so that they could keep up with the action. You can see this when you visit the city of College Station and go by the Lettermen's Association Texas A&M Athletic Sports Museum, located in the Bernard C. Richardson Zone of Kyle Field.

Strange But True!

The Coldest Fight Song in Texas

Winters High School, located in the city of Winters, south of Abilene, has a rather chilly fight song. It seems that the town likes to capitalize on its name; the high school chose "Walkin' in a Winter Wonderland" as its fight song. The high school's team name is likewise cold: the Blizzards.

The town name, incidentally, has nothing to do with cold weather. In 1889, a rancher and land agent by the name of John N. Winters donated some land for a schoolhouse to be built in the area, and when the town got its charter in 1894, town officials named the town after him.

Houston Teams Matchup

See if you can match sport with the team names (answers appear below, but don't peek!). Note that some sports may go with more than one team.

1. Football
2. Hockey
3. Basketball
4. Baseball

a. Houston Astros
b. Houston Rockets
c. Houston Comets
d. Houston Aeros
e. Houston Texans

Answers: 1, e; 2, d; 3, b and c; 4, a.

So . . . Do Ya Feel Lucky?

If you're feeling lucky, you should try your hand at catching some of the big ones in Texas or on the Gulf Coast. From the Gulf of Mexico to the Panhandle, you can try your hand at catching bass, bream, trout, redfish, red snapper, shark, speckled trout, tuna, mahi-mahi, and more. If you like a little competition, the Deep Sea Roundup, held every July in Port Aransas, is the oldest fishing tournament on the entire Gulf Coast.

Speaking of "Port A," as the city is affectionately called, Port Aransas is known as the fishing capital of Texas. Besides the great fishing you can find there virtually year-round, Port Aransas has more fishing tournaments than any other city on the Gulf Coast. Especially during the summer months, you can sign up for an angling tournament nearly every weekend.

Q & A

Q. In what city will you find a collection of Jim Hall Chaparral race cars?

A. In Odessa. These race cars were the pioneers of racing technology and are still in use today.

Q. Also in Odessa, what is the name of the professional hockey team?

A. The Jackalopes

Q. What is the name of the AA-affiliate baseball team in Midland?

A. The Midland Rockhounds.

Q. In what Big Bend Country city are the thermal updrafts so strong that it's a fantastic place for hang gliding?

A. The town of Marfa

Q. What is the name of the restaurant in Van Horn, Texas, that is football broadcaster John Madden's favorite place to eat (while watching football on their big-screen TV)?

A. Chuy's Restaurant. The now-famous Mexican restaurant has even named a room after Madden. Lined with pictures of football players, the room has been dubbed "The John Madden Haul of Fame"—haul because Madden refuses to fly and hauls himself around the country in his tour bus.

Q. What is the name of the AA-affiliate of the Houston Astros Baseball team that is based in Corpus Christi?

A. The Corpus Christi Hooks.

Q. What is the German name of the famous water-amusement park in New Braunfels?

A. Schlitterbahn, meaning "slippery road"

Q. What town is the hometown of Dallas Cowboys icon Bob Lilly?

A. Throckmorton. Incidentally, Lilly now is renowned as a landscape photographer, another talent at which he excels.

Q. Which town has an exhibit on baseball icon Roger Hornsby—who is in both the National Baseball Hall of Fame and the Texas Sports Hall of Fame?

A. Winters, Texas. The exhibit is at the Z.I. Hale Museum.

Q. What city is the home of the Texas Rangers, American League baseball team?

A. Arlington. The Ameriquest Field itself is something to see—it has scads of attractions and entertainment within its borders.

Q. Of what Texas city was famed golfer Ben Hogan a native?

A. Dublin.

Q. What is the name of the AA Texas League baseball team in Fort Worth (affiliated with the Texas Rangers)?

A. Frisco RoughRiders.

Q. Where do the players of the National Hockey League team the Dallas Stars practice?

A. The Dr Pepper StarCenter in Frisco.

Q. Who was the first Texan to be inducted into the National Baseball Hall of Fame?

A. Tris Speaker, who's honored in exhibits at the Hubbard Museum in Hubbard, Texas

Q. To what name was the town of Hilbigville changed to in 1931, and why?

A. The children of the town renamed it Rockne, in honor of Notre Dame coach Knute Rockne, who died in a plane crash in 1931.

Q. What town is home to the Texas Sports Hall of Fame, which contains exhibits honoring such greats as Lee Trevino, George Foreman, and Nolan Ryan?

A. Waco.

Q. What Odessa high school football team was made famous in the movie Friday Night Lights?

A. The Permian Panthers.

THE CIVIL WAR AND TEXAS

If at First You Don't Secede . . .

The State of Texas was just a proverbial babe when a statewide election was held in which the fledgling state seceded from the Union. Texas formally seceded from the Union on March 2, 1861, just 15 years after joining it.

Of course, there's more to this amazing story: Sam Houston, who was governor of Texas at the time of the vote to secede, argued against secession. If Texas seceded and became the seventh state of the Confederacy (as it did), he declared, Texans would come to rue their decision.

In an impassioned speech made in Galveston just days before the Ordinance of Secession passed, Houston pleaded with anyone who would listen: "The North is determined to preserve this Union . . . ," he warned, adding,". . . when they begin to move in a given direction, they move with the steady momentum and perseverance of a mighty avalanche."

His stand cost him dearly: His outspoken beliefs, combined with his refusal to take the oath of allegiance to the new Confederate government, resulted in his removal from office in March 1861. He was replaced by Francis R. Lubbock, a native of South Carolina with a firm belief in the Confederate cause and her ability to prevail.

Fort Mason

In Mason, some reconstructed officers' quarters mark the spot where the original Fort Mason stood. Now primarily a site of crumbling foundations, Fort Mason served as a duty station for such Civil War notables as John Bell Hood and Robert E. Lee.

Battling After the War

The last battle of the Civil War—on land, anyway—was in Texas, and it was actually after the Civil War was officially over. Although General Robert E. Lee had surrendered to General Ulysses S. Grant on April 9, 1865, at the Appomattox Courthouse in Virginia, the war raged on—in parts of Texas, as well as in other pockets of the South.

The Battle of Palmito Ranch, near Brownsville (near the Texas–Mexico border) was the site of the last land battle of (or after?) the Civil War. It happened on May 12, 1865. It's ironic that Confederate soldiers were victorious. There's a historical marker near the site on Texas Highway 4 for you to read more about it.

Texas's Own Confederate Memorial Day

The tradition of honoring the fallen heroes of the Civil War began three years after the war ended, when an organization of Union veterans known as the Grand Army of the Republic established Decoration Day, May 5, 1868, as a time for the entire nation to decorate the graves of the war dead with flowers.

Texas honors its own Confederate soldiers on Confederate Heroes Day every January 19.

Galveston, Port of Fear

On July 2, 1861, the USS South Carolina successfully enforced a blockade of the port of Galveston, thereby making receipt and shipment of goods and supplies—not only for the Confederate Army but also for the citizens of Texas—impossible. By early October 1862, the Port of Galveston was under full federal control.

Their position did not last long: On January 1, 1863, Confederate forces wrested control of the port in the Battle of Galveston. This success too was short-lived—you know the rest of the story. . . .

State Emancipation Proclamation

It was June 19, 1865, that emancipation came to the slaves in Texas. Federal General Gordon Granger, who was then commander of the U.S. forces in Texas, came to Galveston. It was here he proclaimed the Emancipation Proclamation in force for those who were enslaved in the Lone Star State. You probably recall that Lincoln made his official Emancipation Proclamation on January 1, 1863, but Texas celebrates its own special day. Today it is a statewide celebration with parades and other activities as, every year, people in Texas celebrate their own day of freedom for all, calling it Juneteenth.

Incidentally, the place of the first Juneteenth—Ashton Villa in Galveston—is an elegantly restored old Italianate villa, open for tours.

Top Billing

The first woman ever to appear on any American currency appeared on a Confederate States of America $100 bill. That woman was the First Lady of South Carolina, Lucy Holcombe Pickens.

Do you think that when she was growing up in Marshall, Texas, she ever thought, I'd like to be on the $100 bill of the Confederate States of America?

This Texan Was Handy with a Needle

In 1861, a lady by the name of E.A. Coleman wrote her sister that she was creating a flag to represent the Confederacy. In her letter, she described her flag this way:

It has a blue centre with 7 stars of white in a circle and two red and one white stripes. Tomorrow the Legislature of Texas convenes, and it is to be raised tomorrow, as soon as we can get it done. The Lone Star Flag has been flying ever since Lincoln's election was confirmed. We will soon need to add more stars. . . .

Texas Historical Commission historian Willie McWhorter directed me to Julie Holcomb, Director of the Pearce Museum which houses a huge Civil War collection, including Coleman's letter. "This is a significant part of Civil War history," she told me, "that this lady of Texana [Jackson County] was the first designer of the flag of the Confederate States of America." She requests that anyone wanting to see Coleman's letter call them in advance. The Pearce Museum is on the campus of Navarro College in Corsicana, Texas.

John Tyler and the Confederacy's "Last Hope"

In 1863, with the Southern states growing ever more desperate for help in what many Southerners still refer to as the War of Northern Aggression, a man by the name of Major John Tyler was headed to Austin, with a document that, had the timing been better, would have turned the tide of the war. The rest of the Confederates States of America was, by varying degrees, in the hands of Union forces—except for Texas. Major Tyler presented a plan to Texas's Governor Lubbock to save the Confederacy and snatch victory from the very jaws of defeat.

The plan he carried said, in a nutshell, that Texas should appeal to France for aid in beating back the Union

Army. The reason for such a request, said Tyler's missive, was that Texas had been a part of the Louisiana Purchase, a transaction in which France had made certain guarantees.

It remains a mystery why Major Tyler would leave his post in Arkadelphia, Arkansas, and travel 500 miles to Austin on a mission of his own creation. No one knows who actually wrote the rather lengthy missive or who authorized this appeal for aid from France. Governor Lubbock never acted on it, feeling that he should not do so without consulting Jefferson Davis, who was nearing the end of his term as president of the Confederacy.

Had it not been so late in the war and so late in Jefferson Davis's presidency, and had France not been so involved by that point with concerns in Mexico, the end of the war might have been different indeed. Instead, this late-minute appeal, carried by someone without clear authority to do so, remains a minor footnote in the annals of the American Civil War.

Was Tyler the author of this historic yet obscure document? History will never tell us, although the original lies in the Texas State Library and Archives in Austin and is signed "Your Friend, John Tyler, October 27, 1863."

A Tragedy in Gainesville

It was in the fall of 1862, and tensions were high, especially in the South. The Civil War was raging, Galveston was blockaded—and Gainesville was a town of mixed sympathies. Here, neighbor suspected neighbor of being a Union sympathizer. Like a repeat of the Salem witch trials, people blamed others for any problems caused by the Civil War. Gainesville had a sort of witch hunt of its own.

Gainesville is in Cooke County, and Cooke County at that time contained many residents still loyal to the United States. And the Confederate government had promised Texas citizens that they would not be drafted to help in the war effort. They soon broke this promise. Many people loyal to the new Confederate government began to worry that Union sympathizers in Cooke County would not only protest this breach of confidence but would also secede from the Confederacy and rejoin the United States, as several counties already had (in Tennessee).

To prevent anyone from even considering such action, Confederate soldiers rounded up more than 200 suspected Union sympathizers in and around the area of Cooke County in October and tried them for their suspected crime. At least 40 people were hung after being found guilty.

This act struck terror in Cooke County residents, and no one spoke of rejoining the Union afterward.

Today, when you visit Gainesville, you can visit memorials to the Civil War. Stroll the grounds of the courthouse, which has an impressive rotunda. On the grounds themselves is one of the most lavish memorials in Texas, a tribute to the Confederate soldiers, which was erected in the early 1900s by the United Daughters of the Confederacy.

When you read the poetic inscription there, remember also the victims of the tragedy in Gainesville, hung for a crime they perhaps did not commit.

At Half-Mast in Perpetuity

The town of Comfort was just that in 1854, when German settlers, weary from traveling west, settled there as their final destination. The peace they hoped for, however, was short-lived.

When the Civil War broke out and Texas seceded

from the Union, Comfort, as did Gainesville, contained residents who sympathized with the North. When tensions rose to the boiling point, approximately 65 settlers opted to leave, and they headed to Mexico. As the settlers neared Fort Clark, they were surprised by mounted Confederate soldiers. In a brief battle, 19 settlers were killed, and the 9 wounded were executed a few hours after the attack.

A monument in Comfort, Treue Der Union, stands in honor of the settlers who died in that battle, and the U.S. flag that flies over the cemetery is always at half-mast.

Extraordinary Valor: The Story of Edward Smith

Although he was born in Louisiana in 1845, Edward Smith became a Texan when his family moved to Newton County when he was still very young. When the Civil War broke out, 18-year-old Smith enlisted in the Confederate Army. It was then that the Union naval forces threatened the coast of Texas; Smith and his fellow soldiers slogged through the swamplands of East Texas to aid the forces of Lieutenant Richard W. Dowling, where, with only a handful of men, they fought off the invading federal forces.

Union forces were attempting to invade Texas at the site of Sabine Pass. The Union fleet contained 22 vessels and approximately 5,000 soldiers. Smith, Dowling, and their 42 soldiers had as part of their defensive materials the earthen Fort Griffin, containing a mere six cannons.

The Battle of Sabine Pass lasted a mere 45 minutes, during which Dowling and Smith and their handful of men took approximately 350 Union soldiers prisoner, wounded or killed 68 more, and crippled three of the Union Army gunboats. Their victory is all the more amazing considering that the Confederate soldiers had been outnumbered nearly 100 to 1.

According to author Bob Bowman, who writes columns for the online history magazine Texas Escapes, this was the only battle ever fought in East Texas, and even against such military force, the Confederates suffered no losses or injuries. The aftermath of the battle found the remnants of the Union fleet making a hasty retreat to New Orleans.

Courageous soldier that he was, Smith survived the war and eventually became a preacher. He now lies interred in Fairmount Cemetery, alongside many family members. A statue of Richard W. Dowling graces the Sabine Pass Battleground State Park and Historic Site.

Lee to the Rear! Or, Texans Who Probably Saved Their General

In May 1864, in the well-known Battle of the Wilderness, Confederate General Robert E. Lee ordered Hood's Texas Brigade to the front. When the line began to crumble, Hood's Brigade served to reinforce the line; inspired by the men's heroism, General Lee began leading the men in the charge.

Hood's Texas Brigade surrounded Lee, shouting, "Lee to the rear!" and held onto his horse, Traveler, until he followed their orders.

This is said to be one of the more poignant incidents in the Civil War, and although the Texas Brigade suffered losses, the battle resulted in a standstill—with Lee safely in the rear, away from the action.

Incidentally, you can see more about Hood's Texas Brigade at the Texas Heritage Museum in Hillsboro.

Saving Soldiers and Children: Gail Borden

In 1844, a man by the name of Gail Borden was living with his family in Galveston. Borden had always been fascinated with the relationship between dirt, germs, and illness, although during this time, anyone who held beliefs along these lines was thought to have a screw loose (this was before Louis Pasteur).

When a yellow fever epidemic swept through Galveston that year, Borden's young son contracted the disease, succumbing quickly. Sometime afterward, Borden was on a ship after a visit to England and watched as young children aboard ship died from tainted milk, which at the time could not be safely stored or transported.

Borden was resolved to make life healthier and safer for people and began working with milk, trying to create a way to preserve it so it could be safely stored and consumed later. He created a kind of a kettle that he called a vacuum pan, and in 1856, he had perfected canned, condensed milk, which could be stored indefinitely and was safe for infants and children to drink.

In New York, he began operating a milk-condensing plant, and the milk business began to grow. What really sealed the success of Borden's invention was the Civil War: When it broke out, the military used condensed milk to such an extent that Borden couldn't keep up with the demand, and he became quite wealthy. After the war, soldiers told their wives about the canned milk, and it became a pantry staple around the country. His fortunes waxed and waned as Borden tried his hand at other inventions, but none were ever as successful as his Eagle Brand condensed milk.

You know the bovine "spokes-cow" better than you know Gail Borden. Had it not been for a fascination with germs and disease prevention, we would never have met Elsie, the Borden cow—or be enjoying so many dishes made with Borden's milk.

Incidentally, Borden's original vacuum pan is on display in the Agricultural Hall of the National Museum of American History in Washington, D.C., and both the town of Gail, Texas, and Borden County are named in his memory.

The Story of Sibley's Campaign

It was early in the war, and the Confederate government was eyeing the New Mexico Territory, considering taking it and making it part of the Confederate States of America. There were two reasons for this: One was due to its proximity to Texas, and the Southern government did not like all those Union military posts so near its most western Southern state. The other reason was that the territory held promise, with its resources of minerals, land, and people, all of which would help the South.

The first Confederates to attempt this takeover were led by Lieutenant Colonel John R. Baylor, who, along with his men known as the Second Texas Mounted Rifles, was only partially victorious—after all, the territory was vast, and Baylor and his 300 or so men simply couldn't eradicate the Union soldiers by themselves. Confederate President Jefferson Davis then ordered some assistance for Baylor.

That assistance was in the form of General Henry H. Sibley, who organized several regiments in Texas and began heading to the New Mexico Territory. Leading the Fourth, Fifth, and Seventh Texas Mounted Volunteers, Sibley met the men under Baylor's command in El Paso, where they were incorporated into the newly formed brigade.

At first, Sibley and his men followed the course of the Rio Grande, heading north, and were victorious at Valverde (February 21, 1862). On March 28, he led his men in a struggle in the Battle of Glorieta Pass, in which both sides claimed victory. Victory or not, the Confederate's supply train was destroyed, all their reserves gone. Dispirited, Sibley and his men returned to Texas, their goal unrealized, with the New Mexico Territory remaining in the hands of the Union.

Strange But True!

The Mystery of the Dead Man's Hole

Slightly northwest of Austin is the town of Marble Falls, which has as part of its folklore and creepy legend a spot called Dead Man's Hole. Located off County Road 401, Dead Man's Hole is a 155-foot-deep fissure in the Earth that opens up into a wide cave near the bottom. What it was used for during the Civil War is what, some say, has made it a haunted place even today.

The hole was first discovered in 1821 by a German entomologist doing research in the area. Luckily, he didn't fall in, but Union sympathizers during Civil War weren't so lucky: As many as 17 such victims fell prey to gravity and died at the bottom of the pit.

Although the bodies were recovered after the war was over, the presence of foul and toxic gases prevented exploration of the pit. After the gases dissipated in 1951, some cave-explorers (called spelunkers) from the University of Texas explored the pit and discovered it to be seven feet in diameter at its opening and nearly 160 feet deep, with two further caverns, one extending 15 feet horizontally and another extending about 30 feet at a 45-degree angle.Is Dead Man's Hole haunted by the ghosts of Union sympathizers? Columnist Mike Cox, who writes for Texas Escapes, thinks it's a possibility. He explored the area and wrote about it.

In 1999, the land surrounding the pit was deeded to Burnet County for use as a park. Ghost hunters (that is, paranormal researchers) with the Austin Paranormal Society claim that since then, there has been evidence of ghostly activity around the site, but the hole itself cannot be explored: Years ago, the opening was sealed with a heavy metal grate.

You can visit the park and see the opening of the hole, however. About the time the area became a park, the state also erected a historical marker, telling the eerie story of one of Marble Falls' claims to fame.

Round-Robin Frontier Patrols

After Texas seceded from the Union and joined the Confederacy, Union soldiers were relieved of their duties, so to speak, along the Texas frontier, and Texas and the Confederacy were obliged to take over this role. The First Regiment, known as the Texas Mounted Riflemen, began patrolling the frontier in early 1861 until their enlistment was over in April 1862. They were said to have been an effective deterrent against Indian raids in the line of forts ranging from the Red River to the Rio Grande.

Those men must have been a tough act to follow, for when the Frontier Regiment replaced the First Regiment, despite establishing 16 encampments at 25-mile intervals along the frontier, their movements became much too predictable for the roaming Indian tribes, and attacks only increased. In March 1864, the Frontier Organization, formed of local groups of men, replaced the Frontier Regiment. For a time, it seemed this group could be successful in deterring Indian attacks, but later that same year, when Kiowa and Comanche warriors fell upon a group of Texans along Elm Creek (Young County), there were more Texans dead than Indian (one Kiowa in particular, Chief Satanta, gained significant notoriety in raiding Texas settlements).

These increasingly vicious attacks did not inspire soldiers to focus their efforts in protecting the local people; they seemed more inclined to pursue deserters and monitor federal activities rather than protect their own.

The Curse of Maximilian's Treasure

This story actually had its origins just after the Civil War, but because some of its characters are Confederate soldiers, it seems to belong in this chapter.

Somewhere between the town of Odessa and Crane, you might be the lucky one to locate an imperial treasure worth more than $15 million. If you can't locate the treasure, you can find, in either of these towns, someone who can tell you all about the legend, the curse—and the treasure. The legend goes something like this:

When America was in the throes of the Civil War, France (specifically, Charles-Louis-Napoléon Bonaparte, Napoléon Bonaparte's nephew) decided they would also reach out for more countries to rule. That country was Mexico, and Austrian Ferdinand Joseph Maximilian was chosen to rule as its emperor, and his wife, Charlotte (a Belgian princess), was to rule as empress. France invaded Mexico, but it took the French Army more than a year to overthrow the government. Finally, in 1864, Maximilian and his wife took their thrones, with the support of the Mexican wealthy.

They were apparently despotic rulers, snatching all the wealth that was dug out of Mexican mines. They amassed a fortune in gold and jewels while ignoring the needs of the people, and Mexicans were becoming resentful of being ruled by an Austrian emperor and the French Army. After two years, Maximilian's and Charlotte's standing with even the wealthy Mexicans was precarious at best.

Their rule coming to an end, Maximilian decided to smuggle his Mexican-gained wealth back to Austria. He had his servants load 15 wagons full of gold and silver coins, jewelry, and fine china, and shipped these wagons out of Mexico, accompanied by 15 Mexican teamsters and some Austrian soldiers. Maximilian had a plan: sneak his treasure not out of a port in Mexico (where it was sure to be discovered and seized) but out of one in Texas, such as Galveston. He stayed on in Mexico, encouraged by supporters to think that he could keep the throne, but sent his treasure, disguised as flour, north.

The small wagon train successfully crossed the border into Texas at Presidio, north of the Mexican state of Chihuahua. Once in Texas, the party met a group of Confederate soldiers. They told the soldiers that they were from Missouri but were headed to Mexico. They were hired to help guard the "flour."

As anyone would, the Confederates got suspicious. Taking a peek inside a wagon one night, they discovered the truth, and then greed got the best of them. It is said that the next night, the Confederates shot and killed all 15 Mexican teamsters and the Austrian guards. This happened at a place called Castle Gap, which lies between Crane and Upton Counties.

The half-dozen Confederates decided to bury the treasure—after all, they couldn't manage moving the 15 wagons themselves—and to dig it up when things settled down. They buried the treasure, throwing the 19 bodies on top, then burned the wagons over the disturbed ground. Anyone seeing the area would think that nothing more than the wagons had burned. They turned the oxen loose to fend for themselves. All 6 Confederates did carry some of the treasure with them in their saddlebags, and that is where the curse of the treasure comes in.

One of the men claimed sickness and said he'd stay behind, but the other five got suspicious. Thinking that he planned on going back for the treasure himself, they shot him and left him for dead.

The sixth Confederate wasn't dead, however. He managed to walk and was headed toward San Antonio when he found the bodies of his former compatriots. They had been killed, and their saddlebags were empty.

The last living survivor of the treasure wagon train knew that his own moments were numbered. Eventually he found a doctor, but his wound was infected and it was too late. He drew a map and gave it to the doctor. Neither the doctor nor anyone else has ever found the treasure.

As for the former Mexican rulers, the French Army left Mexico in 1867, Maximilian was executed, Benito Juárez was named president, and Charlotte died in a mental institution in Austria.

If you found the treasure, would you be touched by its curse, as everyone else has been? The world may never know, for it's still there, somewhere between Odessa and Crane.

Longhorn Cavern—More Than a Cave

The town of Burnet is home to one of the oldest geological formations in the world. The cave there, which is today part of Longhorn Cavern State Park, stretches underground for two miles. In prehistoric times it was used as a shelter for early humans. During the Civil War, however, it was employed for something much more incendiary—it was the place where gunpowder was secretly made for the Confederate Army. During and after that time, it was also a hangout for outlaws on the run, but today it is the place for history buffs to connect with the past.

If you are into the Civil War or are a spelunking or a geology enthusiast, you don't want to miss Longhorn Cavern State Park, or nearby White Bluff, while you're in town.

Q & A

Q. What was the largest prisoner of war camp west of the Mississippi, once used for Union prisoners of war?

A. Camp Ford, in Tyler. The camp contains replicas of prisoner cabins and is open for tours.

Q. Where will you find the grave of the last survivor of the Civil War?

A. A few miles southeast of the town of Franklin, Walter Williams is buried in the cemetery at Mount Pleasant Church.

Q. What Texas town was the site of a pistol factory that produced the Colt .44 "Dragoon" revolver?

A. Lancaster. There is an exhibit of the Confederate States of America foundry in the town library.

Q. Who was known as the tallest soldier of the Confederacy? How tall was he?

A. Henry Clay Thurston of Mount Vernon, who stood 7 feet 7½ inches tall

WHEELERS AND DEALERS

It's a Bird! It's a Plane! It's . . . the Most Successful Commercial Airline in History!

In 1971 two men, Rollin King and Herb Kelleher, got together and shared their vision of starting an airline. They didn't want just any airline—they wanted one that would, amazingly, get passengers where they wanted to go, when they wanted to get there, and show them a wonderful time in the process.

I remember watching the news in 1971, when media covered the launching of Southwest Airlines. Then, it was a modest, three-jet business, with service between its home base of Dallas to Houston and to San Antonio. The news depicted a typical flight as fun—what a difference!— but from the newsman's tone, it was clear he thought that the fledgling airline couldn't last long because it was based on making customers happy.

Southwest Airlines, however, was successful from the beginning, and for those of you who haven't yet flown on its planes yet, the company has tried to make travelers more than just comfortable. Attendants are warm and friendly and at times have seemed to me more like stand-up comedians than flight attendants.

The airline has had such success, as a matter of fact, that it has won more awards for customer service, luggage handling, and on-time arrivals and departures than any other U.S. commercial airline. While they're having fun and being successful, they're also watching out for their passengers—Southwest Airlines flies more than 80 million passengers a year to at least 60 U.S. cities and has the safest record of any commercial airline to date—zero fatalities since the day they first got off the ground in 1971.

I'd say that's pretty amazing. And no, they didn't put me up to this—they didn't even give me a discount while I was flying around Texas, researching this book.

Southwest has created many commemorative airplanes, such as those to honor states and their employees. One of the more unusual ones is Slam Dunk One, which is a salute to and acknowledgment of the airline's partnership with the National Basketball Association.

DID YOU KNOW?

American Airlines

In 1930, more than 80 small airlines incorporated themselves and became American Airways. The name was changed to American Airlines in 1934. In Fort Worth, they recognize and honor this part of their history with the American Airlines C.R. Smith Museum. C.R. Smith is called the "Father of American Airlines."

Texas Tidbits

Texas is home to not only Dell and Compaq but also many other high-tech industries. Central Texas has so many high-tech businesses in its area that it is called the Silicon Valley of the South.

Dallas is where the store chains Neiman Marcus and JCPenney were founded, and the Federal Reserve Bank of Dallas, one of 12 banks in the Federal Reserve System, was also founded there. Snack food giant Frito Lay has its home office outside Dallas (Plano).

Also in Dallas, the State Fair of Texas attracts more than 3 million visitors (along with their wallets) every year.

You'd Have to Go to Egypt to See More Pyramids!

The late Texas entrepreneur W.L. Moody Jr. created a business empire in Galveston during his lifetime and established many beautiful attractions for the area. His former home is now open to the public as the Moody Mansion and Museum, and the Moody Foundation created a series of gardens by the same name.

The Moody Gardens consists of 156 acres with three unique pyramids. The Aquarium Pyramid holds nearly 2 million gallons of water, which exhibits ocean habitats from around the world. The 10-story-tall Rainforest Pyramid is a delight for those who love rain forests and even has a bat cave. The Discovery Pyramid is a glass pyramid and is for those who love space exploration and the thrills it offers.

All Pumped Up

The town of Electra, named after the daughter of circa-1900s cattle baron W.T. Waggoner, was officially named the Pump Jack Capital of Texas by the Texas Legislature in 2001. Beginning with its first oil gusher in 1911 (Clayco Number 1), this North Texas town continues to produce voluminous amounts of the stuff—within a 10-mile radius of Electra today, there are about 5,000 pumping units, working constantly. To celebrate their designation, the city hosts its annual Pump Jack Festival every April.

Feeling a Little Crazy? Try a Visit to Mineral Wells

In 1885, a well of mineral water was discovered in the town of Mineral Wells on the Panhandle Plains. This wasn't just any mineral water—it was named Crazy Well, and people claimed it could cure mental illnesses, among other diseases. Word spread like wildfire on a prairie in a high wind, and the little settlement known as Mineral Wells became nationally famous.

In 1904, entrepreneur Edward P. Dismuke founded the Famous Mineral Water Company, which bottled, sold, and distributed the famous healing water. The bottler is still in business under the same name. You can visit the bottler, relax in its pavilion, read the historical marker at the site, have ice cream and coffee, sample different kinds of mineral waters, and tour the garden full of native Texas fauna.

You Haven't Been to the Largest Honky-Tonk in the World?

You just have to visit Billy Bob's Texas in Fort Worth. It has more than 7,000 combined square feet of a rodeo area, bar rails, and stage area for entertainment.

These Boots Were Made for Walking

The boot-making capital of Texas is El Paso. The city is home to many boot-making companies, including J.B. Hill, Lucchese, Rocketbuster, and others. Tony Lama, probably the oldest such company in town, started making its boots there in 1911.

A New Kind of Iron Horse

In 1995, Bill Rucker and Tim Edmondson had a dream: create a company for building custom motorcycles. They opened American IronHorse Motorcycle Co. in Fort Worth, and today create everyone else's dream custom cycles in their 224,000-square-foot factory.

The company has grown to be the nation's largest producer of V-twin custom motorcycles.

When the Going Gets Tough, the Tough Make Baseball Gloves

The Nocona-based company called Nocona Leather Goods Company was doing a pretty fair business until the Great Depression, but then it was unable to sell its products—mostly purses and billfolds—so it started making baseball gloves, changing its name to Nocona Athletic Goods Company.

Decades later, the Nocona ball glove is still a prize catch, and the company also produces boots, saddles, and sporting goods. I guess that when they hit on this idea, it just kind of caught on. . . .

Doing Business the Old-Fashioned Way

The movie Field of Dreams had as one of its key lines "If you build it, he will come." The tiny city of Baird, 20 miles from Austin, decided to make itself into an antiques capital. Although there were no antiques shops in Baird at the time, that didn't stop the townsfolk. They got busy getting such shops into the city.

Sure enough, during the state legislative session of June 1993, Baird was named the official Antique Capital of West Texas. The plan worked: For its size (a population of approximately 1,800), the city is chock-full of antique shops—more than 20 antique malls and 100 antique dealers (so far).

The Front Camps

The lumber business has always been a big part of the Texas economy. During the late 1800s and nearly to the mid-1900s, sawmill towns were a way of life for many lumber workers and their families.

The towns had names such as Bluff City, Lindsey

Springs, and Alceda and were mobile logging camps, complete with everything the workers and their families might need. The best-remembered one is Fastrill, which was named after three lumber company officials (Farrington, Strauss, and Hill). Fastrill lasted until 1941, and like other front camps (so called because they were situated at the front, or edge, of forested land), it was situated in areas as long as the timber was there; then it was moved in its entirety to another forested area of Texas.

Now, the only reminders of the front camps are trails and forest clearings. But the memories of them live on in the minds of those who worked and lived in them.

You can see more about the history of forestry in Texas at the Texas Forestry Museum in Lufkin, which has, as part of its ever-expanding exhibits, a sawmill town.

Cereal on the Level(land)

Cereal king C.W. Post made his home in Levelland, which he surveyed and plotted himself, in 1912.

Aunt Jemima

The last live model who was Quaker Oats Company's Aunt Jemima was Rosie Lee Moore of Hearne, Texas. She actively toured as Aunt Jemima during the 1950s and 1960s. She passed away in 1967 and now lies interred in the Hammond Colony Cemetery just northeast of town.

Where "How May I Help You?" Has Been Said Longer Than Anywhere Else in Texas

In the town of Belton, north of Austin, is a store that has as its claim to fame of being the oldest department store in Texas. Cochran, Blair & Potts was first opened in 1869 by a former Confederate colonel by the name of H.M. Cook. The store's president is now Cook's great-great-

great-grandson, Robert Roy Potts.

The store is so ancient that you can still see the square hole cut in the ceiling, which store clerks used for sending the money from their tills from the store floor— via basket—to the offices on the second floor. The store is located at 221 East Central Avenue. They no longer use the basket method—they are modern but still have that old-time friendliness that's kept them in business since 1869.

The (Sweet) Story of Blue Bell Creamery

My son Gus loves Blue Bell ice cream, and with good reason: It's the best we've ever tasted, and that's why it's still around. The Brenham Creamery Company was founded in 1907, and then the company changed its name to Blue Bell Creameries in honor of the many bluebell flowers to be found in and around the city of Brenham.

They're still operating as they did back in 1907, though, and the employees are as friendly as any you'll find. They're open for tours and, of course, tastings.

Blue Jeans Capital of the World?

Cotton is one of the main crops in the town of Littlefield. That particular king provides the local mill with enough material to make 19 million pairs of blue jeans annually!

The Texas Inventor of the Hamburger

An ambitious entrepreneur named Fletcher Davis was a food vendor on the courthouse square in Athens, Texas. It is said that he created a meat-patty sandwich between two buns for those hungry courthouse workers and others in the downtown area. It was such a popular staple that he and his friend from Ohio, Frank Menches, attended the 1904 World's Fair in St. Louis, Missouri, and introduced their invention—the hamburger—to the hungry public.

Other people have also claimed to be the inventor of the hamburger, but for the people of Athens, Texas, Davis is the guy, hands—er, patties—down.

Putting a (Beautiful) Face on Business

A young woman from Houston, born Mary Kathlyn Wagner, had three small children to support. She was great at sales and knew it but was taking premed courses toward a medical degree. Her mother had always told her, "You can do it!" and that had been her life's motto.

Then the girl who had always won everything she had set out for had a setback: In taking an aptitude test, she learned that she wasn't cut out much for medicine. Instead, she showed a great aptitude for sales. Was life handing her lemonade? Apparently the young mother of three decided that it was showing her a different path to take in her life, for she began working in sales, first for a company called Stanley Home Products, then for a company called World Gift.

The mature woman retired after 25 years as a highly successful saleswoman—then, after a month, realized retirement wasn't for her. After writing a successful how-to marketing book especially for women, she decided to apply those principles to her own sales life. She bought a formula for a skin cream and opened her own company. Tragedy struck when her husband died a month before the launching of her company. The budding entrepreneur had second thoughts but then realized this was her one chance, so she implemented her plan.

Fast-forward to today. The woman who would have continued in premed had it not been for that aptitude test has become one of the icons of the business world. Now people the world over know of Mary Kay cosmetics, and the company today is one of the largest privately held firms in the country, with sales in excess of $2.2 billion.

Her son, Chairman and CEO Richard Rogers, says his mother's faith in people is what made the company so uniquely hers, and although she passed away at Thanksgiving in 2001, her legacy of believing in others and in oneself lives on.

Now, you can tour the Mary Kay Museum in Addison, and guided tours are available. The corporate office is in nearby Dallas.

Thanks to a woman with a vision and strong belief in herself, pink Cadillacs are a part of the American culture (Mary Kay sales associates can earn the right to lease a Mary Kay car, often a pink Cadillac), and women have more confidence in their abilities and have more control of their lives.

Six Flags, Texas's Theme Park

Located in Arlington, Six Flags Over Texas is definitely one of the biggest draws for families who visit, and with good reason: It's just plain nonstop excitement. Here are some facts about Six Flags Over Texas, from its official Web site (see "Virtual Texas" near the back of this book for the address):

• The park's roller coasters travel 2.5 million miles each year.

• The company has more roller coasters than any other theme-park companies in the world—combined.

• Six Flags Over Texas is the largest theme-park company in the world.

• Six Flags Over Texas was the first Six Flags theme park ever.

- The company is philanthropic, serving ill children through the Children's Miracle Network.
- The company has been in the fun-making business since 1961.

The World's Oldest Major Soft Drink and Its Creators

Research has told us that our sense of smell has more connections to memory than any other of our senses. One man's olfactory nerve led him to re-create a memory of his own—but that's getting ahead (or a-nose) of the story.

The story begins with a young pharmacist by the name of Charles Alderton, who worked at Morrison's Old Corner Drug Store in Waco. Although his main job as a pharmacist was mixing concoctions to ease people's ills, he was fascinated with the many fruit and spice smells in the drugstore—a blend of what emitted from the soda fountain and candies. Alderton began testing different flavors, trying to recreate the taste of what his nose told him, and after a number of experiments, came up with what he thought was the perfect mixture of fruit syrups.

The drugstore owner was the first to sample the new drink, and liked it; then fountain customers did likewise, with the same response. After a while, Alderton's mixture became so popular that locals came in just to order a drink they dubbed the "Waco."

That was in 1885. Dr Pepper, as we know it (and as Morrison is said to have named it), was later developed by Morrison and a beverage chemist by the name of Robert S. Lazenby under the company name of Artesian Manufacturing and Bottling Company (which later became the Dr Pepper Company), and in 1904 they introduced Dr Pepper to the world—or at least the 20 million or so people who attended the 1904 World's Fair in St. Louis. Hailed as the "king of beverages" in its early days, Dr Pepper was also hailed as a kind of health drink—to be consumed at those "sinking spell" times of day (thus the slogan and logo, "10, 2 and 4").

Now you can tour the Dr Pepper Museum on 5th Street in Waco, where an animated mannequin resembling Charles Alderton gives a little speech on the origins of his famous drink. The museum is filled with all types of Dr Pepper memorabilia, including mouse pads and refrigerator magnets.

By the way, the claim of being the location of the oldest Dr Pepper bottler in the world is held by Dublin, Texas, which changes its name to "Dr Pepper, Texas" every year in June for the annual Dr Pepper celebration. The bottling plant opened there in 1891, six years after the invention of Dr Pepper in Waco.

Thanks to Alderton's incredible olfactory nerve, Texas has yet another claim to fame.

The Story of Gladys's Fruitcakes and the World's Largest Fruitcake

There's always a joke about fruitcakes going around, particularly during the Christmas holidays, but one taste of a fruitcake from Gladys' Bakery might change your mind. Czechoslovakian Texan Gladys Farek Holub started out first making homemade bread for local restaurants in the area south of Austin, then made cookies and other confections, and finally decided to try her hand at making fruitcakes.

These wouldn't be just any old fruitcake, with the usual spices, raisins, dates, and citron—she wanted to make a fruitcake so loaded with fresh, local pecans that they needed only a little batter to hold 'em together.

At first, Gladys made small batches, but everything

was snapped up rapidly. Then she was inspired: She would not only make the world's largest fruitcake but also make it in the shape of Texas, where everything is bigger anyway! Gladys purchased a brand-new stainless-steel cement mixer and began mixing and making the huge fruitcakes. Her attempts were a huge success: Gladys's world's largest fruitcakes not only are delicious but also weigh an average of 150 pounds and measure five by six feet. She has appeared on the Tonight Show and the Late Show with David Letterman, among others, and she sent one of her huge fruitcakes to troops in Iraq during Operation Desert Storm in the early 1990s. It was reported that 7,000 soldiers ate that fruitcake in about 45 minutes.

The World's Largest Fruitcake, with Gladys. Courtesy Gladys' Bakery.

You can order fruitcakes, cookies, and other goodies (all normal size) via her Web site. If you want to really impress someone, though, the World's Largest Fruitcake would definitely get someone's attention.

Gladys's business continues to grow, and although Gladys is retired, her daughter Melissa Varley has taken over the reins . . . er . . . mixer and continues the tradition of making fruitcakes and other confections big on taste and everything else.

To visit the bakery, you'll want to go to the town of Dubina, although the company's mailing address is in Weimar. See "Virtual Texas" at the back of this book for the Web site's address.

The Story of the "World's Finest Innkeeper"

On what used to be Avenue D in the small town of Cisco, there was a small inn called the Mobley Hotel, built for Henry Mobley in 1916.

Once the oil boom in Texas started, everyone caught oil fever. Henry Mobley had it as bad as everyone else, it seems. In 1919, his inn was full of people who were out to get rich quick in the oil boom that was at its apex in west central Texas. So high was the demand for a place to sleep that Mobley turned his 40-room hotel into one that would accommodate several times that number. He began renting his rooms in eight-hour shifts that coincided with those of the oil-field workers.

That same year, a young banker came to town to purchase a bank there, but the deal fell through. Discouraged, he sought out a room to stay the night and arrived at the Mobley Hotel.

When he discovered Henry Mobley's quick-turnover room rental structure, he made Mobley an offer to buy the hotel then and there, for $40,000. Mobley, in the grip of oil fever, agreed, and the young banker was suddenly an innkeeper. That night—according to the historical marker in front of the hotel—the young banker-turned-innkeeper dreamed of a chain of his hotels scattered across Texas. He immediately began making changes to the hotel, based on a philosophy of "maximum cost and maximum comfort," and was the first to create a shop in a hotel, starting a trend that is still popular today.

Although the new innkeeper sold his hotel in 1929, his flair for hotel administration and hospitality became the benchmark by which all hotels today are judged. The man himself is known as the father of the hospitality industry. The banker-turned-innkeeper was Conrad Hilton, and today there are hundreds of Hilton Hotels around the world.

Oh, in case you're wondering what became of the first hotel, it went through several iterations (an apartment building, a senior citizens' home, and such) before being transferred by Eric Hilton to the University of Houston Foundation. In 1979—the year of Conrad Hilton's death— the University of Houston (which, incidentally, is the site of the Conrad N. Hilton College of Hotel and Restaurant Management) designated the Mobley Hotel as a memorial museum dedicated to honor the man who was "the worlds' finest innkeeper."

Q & A

Q. What pioneering couple on the Gulf Coast started the first rum distillery in Texas?

A. Martin and Elizabeth Varner. Their property was last privately owned by the first native-born Texas governor, James Stephen Hogg. The mansion, today known as the Varner-Hogg Plantation, is now a State Historic Site, located just outside West Columbia, and is open for tours.

Q. What area in Galveston was once known as the Wall Street of the Southwest?

A. The Strand, which was a commercial district at one time. Restored to its former grandeur, this section of the city, with its collection of 1800s-era buildings, has a wonderful selection of art galleries, pubs, and studios.

Q. What shrimp trawler that worked the Gulf of Mexico more than 25 years is now on display as part of an exhibit celebrating the shrimping industry in Freeport (Brazosport harbor channel)?

A. Now a shrimp-boat monument, the trawler Mystery is forever moored as an educational tourist exhibit.

Q. Who began the Brotherhood of Timber Workers in East Texas, a short-lived union of sawmill workers when sawmill camps were at their heyday (1880–1940)?

A. John Henry Kirby

Q. In what town was a storekeeper who, taking advantage of the fact that his store straddled the Texas–Louisiana state border, sold liquor on one side and allowed gambling on the other?

A. Bethany

Q. What was the city that had its beginnings in a real-estate deal, when the Allen Brothers landed in a place on the coast called Buffalo Bayou?

A. The city of Houston

Q. What town has established an "Old World shopping experience," where you can feel as though you are in Venice, Italy?

A. The city of Shenandoah. The area has 10 waterfalls and fountains.

THE FILM, MUSIC, AND DRAMA OF TEXAS

If the Real Alamo Is Too Crowded for You . . .

If the crowds of tourists in San Antonio get to be too much, you might want to try a visit to the city of Brackettville, east of Del Rio. Craftsmen from Mexico created an adobe replica of the Alamo for the filming of the movie *The Alamo* in 1959. Featuring John Wayne at his best, the movie set still exists in this town. You can tour the replica of the famous battle site, complete with an 1800s-era frontier village—and maybe watch another movie or commercial being filmed, as "Alamo Village" is put to proper use from time to time today.

In the summer months you can also see mock shoot-outs between frontier reenactors in the streets, and enjoy country and Western shows in this town that takes you back in time.

Goin' to (Little) Graceland . . .

You might find yourself humming the tune "Goin' to Graceland" as you drive to Los Fresnos (just north of Brownsville), for it is here you will find Little Graceland. Retired soldier Simon Vega served with the King when they were stationed together in Germany, and in him, Elvis Presley had a lifelong fan.

Little Graceland is chock-full of memorabilia relating to the King, with lots of photographs, posters, and even one of Elvis's Good Conduct Medals when he was in the army (he gave it to Vega). The front of Vega's house resembles the mansion in Memphis, complete with white wrought-iron gate; Vega is also in the midst of building a replica of Elvis's birthplace (Tupelo, Mississippi) in his yard. Little Graceland is open for tours, and every August (the month of Elvis's death), Vega holds Elvis impersonator contests.

DID YOU KNOW?

A Real Swinger

The town that has as its claim to fame as home to the king of Western swing is Turkey. Musician Bob Wills (1905–1975) was raised on a farm nearby, and the town has a museum as well as a monument in his honor. On the last Saturday of every April, the city holds a Bob Wills Reunion, but in 2005, the event was expanded: Cities, radio stations, and other entertainment venues celebrated Wills's 100th birthday with all kinds of live music. The Texas Lottery Commission did even more: It created a scratch-off lottery ticket with his picture on it. This was the first time in Texas lottery history that someone's image had appeared on a lottery ticket.

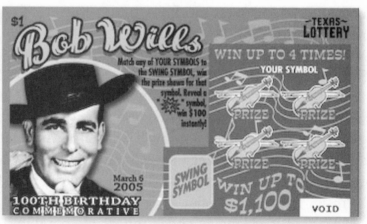

Bob Wills is the first person to have his image on a Texas Lottery ticket. Courtesy Texas Lottery Commission.

Bob—and his Texas Playboys—would have been proud.

Viva Texas!

The 1952 film *¡Viva Zapata!* (with Marlon Brando, Anthony Quinn, and Jean Peters) was filmed not in Mexico but in the town of Roma, Texas, because it looked like such an authentic old-Mexico town. The story, authored by John Steinbeck, was about Mexican revolutionary Emiliano Zapata, who led a rebellion against President Porfirio Díaz in the early nineteenth century. Imagine living there then, rubbing elbows with such big names!

For Dale Watson Fans . . .

If you're in Austin on a Thursday or Sunday evening and want to try your luck at hearing musician Dale Watson, he'll be playing at Ginny's Little Longhorn Saloon on Burnet Road (the song "Turn On the Jukebox, Ginny" was written about this place) if he's in town. Even if he's not there, you can look over the awards he has won, which are displayed on a wall behind the bar.

Besides offering you the opportunity to listen to Watson's live music, Ginny's give you the chance to play Chicken Poop Bingo on Sunday afternoon (see Chapter 12, "Food and Fascinating Cultural Tidbits," for more on this story).

The Krayolas, the Tex-Mex Beatles. Courtesy Hector Saldana, singer with The Krayolas.

"Tex-Mex Beatles"

The big collector craze is a type of music called power pop. The Krayolas have been big into power pop. In 2007 they released a 16-song collection entitled *Best Riffs Only*. The music, according to guitarist Hector Saldana, can best be described as "Tex-Mex Beatles."

Well, if you love it, you know it can't be bad. . . .

Are We in Nashville?

The town of Carthage is proud to claim one of its native sons as Tex Ritter, the famous "singing cowboy." The town celebrates his legend in the form of its Texas Country Music Hall of Fame and Tex Ritter Museum. There are exhibits there on music icons such as Waylon Jennings, Willie Nelson, Gene Autry, and more.

Visiting this place might make you feel that it's unnecessary to go to Nashville.

Guess Who?

One of the greatest jazz trombonists of all time was born in 1905 in the tiny town of Vernon, Texas (population about 12,000). He began playing professionally while still a teenager, first performing at San Antonio's Horn Palace before joining the Paul Whiteman Band. He went on to record with jazz greats Louis Armstrong and Benny Goodman.

Who was he? Jack Teagarden.

Guess Who Jr.?

Born in Corsicana, the young man had a penchant for music, playing guitar at an early age. He's best known for his 1972 country music hit, "If You've Got the Money, Honey, I've Got the Time." His nickname came from a schoolyard scrap when he was young.

Given up? This was the late Lefty Frizzell. Corsicana honors his memory with the Lefty Frizzell Country Music Museum, open to the public.

Guess Who III?

What musician graduated from Gallatin High School in East Texas and made the song "Honky-Tonk Man" famous and also sang "North to Alaska," which became the title song for the movie by the same name (starring John Wayne and Stewart Granger)?

He was Johnny Horton. He died in November 1960, in Milano, Texas, the victim of an automobile accident.

Texas's Answer to Tennessee's Grand Ole Opry

If you go to Lake Jackson (on the Gulf Coast), you're likely to hear something that will make you think you're in Nashville's Grand Ole Opry. Or at least you will if you go to the Lake Theatre, which hosts weekly musical shows rivaling what you might see and hear in the Volunteer State (hey, they even throw in a magic show!).

The Fort Griffin Fandangle—a Town Event

The city of Albany has as part of its annual traditions, a June gala celebrating its history. That in itself isn't amazing: what's amazing is that more than 200 of the city's population participate in the Fort Griffin Fandangle, as they call it—roughly one fifth of the town's 2,000 inhabitants.

Harmony in Big Bend Country

Born in Austria, Nick Mersfelter could play virtually any instrument known to man. He lived in Fort Davis and served not only as a local music provider but also as the area barber and justice of the peace. For a time he was even a member of the San Antonio Philharmonic Orchestra.

Mersfelter is long gone, but what remains is the Overland Trail Museum, which was his former home. A fascinating piece of Texas history, the museum contains artifacts from the early days of the area—and from the days when Mersfelter's music could be heard by the locals, after they were married or got a haircut.

Musicians and Entertainers Matching Game

Match the descriptions given below with the proper singer, entertainer, or actor (answers below, but don't peek!).

1. Born in 1914 in Crisp, Texas; joined the Grand Ole Opry in 1943. His band was the Texas Troubadours; a record shop still exists that he began. Probably most famous for his songs "Walkin' the Floor Over You" and "Waltz Across Texas."

2. This country music star, a Beaumont native, recently rerecorded the 1970s hit "Before the Next Tear Drop Falls" with the original singer, Freddy Fender. His own first hit single was in 1993: "What's It to You?"

3. She was Roy Rogers's sidekick and made the song "Happy Trails" famous.

4. Born in 1931 in Saratoga, Texas, he sang on the streets of Beaumont when he was just a kid. Probably best loved for the 1980s hit "He Stopped Loving Her Today."

5. This classical pianist was born in Louisiana in 1934 but moved to Texas at the age of six. Played Carnegie Hall in 1948 and in 1958 won the first Tchaikovsky International Competition in Moscow. He founded an international music competition in 1962, which is held in Fort Worth every four years.

6. This singer, born in 1934 in Port Arthur, was smitten with the blues at an early age. Probably her most famous album is Pearl and is probably best known for the song, "Me and Bobby McGee." She died of a heroin overdose at the age of 27.

7. This Beaumont native got his start in that town and signed with MCA Nashville in 1989. His first single was "Too Cold at Home." Born in 1953, he started recording at the age of 17.

8. This man was born in 1907 in Carthage with the last name of Woodward. Initially on a career path to become a lawyer, he became fascinated with cowboy ballads

and acting and was a star on both the stage and screen.

9. Born in Seminole, Texas, this singer had her first country hit in 1972 and became famous for her song "Delta Dawn."

10. Born in 1948 in Houston, she was inducted into the Grand Ole Opry in 1972. One of her best-known songs is "I Was Country When Country Wasn't Cool."

11. Singer from Pleasanton who has sold more than 57 million records, ranking fourth in sales after Elvis Presley, the Beatles, and Barbra Streisand. This singer has had more hit singles than any other country music artist.

12. Born in Houston, probably best known for the songs that propelled him to stardom: "Reuben James" and "Ruby, Don't Take Your Love to Town." He's also a photographer and book author.

13. This singer's given first name was Alvis, born in Sherman in 1929. He was nicknamed after a mule on the family farm and teamed with Roy Clark to host the television show Hee Haw. He opened the Crystal Palace in Bakersfield, California.

14. This singer was born in 1936 in Fort Worth, best known for his 1965 hit, "King of the Road." It has been said that Johnny Cash compared this singer's vocal range to his. He died in 1992.

15. Born in Littlefield, Texas, in 1937, played bass with Buddy Holly. Gave up his seat on the doomed flight that took Holly's life. In 1985, recorded "Highwayman" with Willie Nelson, Johnny Cash, and Kris Kristofferson. He died in 2002.

16. This man was known as the original "singing cowboy." He was also famous for singing "Rudolph, the Red-Nosed Reindeer," among other songs.

17. This singer and actor has been in more than a dozen movies and earned additional fame for being mar-

ried to actress Julia Roberts in the 1990s. His most well-known album is The Road to Ensenada, which won a Grammy in 1996.

18. Born in Carthage, he was a pitcher with the St. Louis Cardinals until an injury sidelined him; then he began playing guitar. He's best known for the song "Have I Told You Lately That I Love You?" Killed in a plane crash in 1964, the town remembers him with a memorial a few miles east of downtown.

a. Gene Autry	j. George Jones
b. Dale Evans	k. George Strait
c. Tex Ritter	l. Van Cliburn
d. Ernest Tubb	m. Kenny Rogers
e. Tanya Tucker	n. Roger Miller
f. Clay Walker	o. Buck Owens
g. Mark Chesnutt	p. Janis Joplin
h. Barbara Mandrell	q. Lyle Lovett
i. Waylon Jennings	r. Jim Reeves

Answers: 1, d; 2, f; 3, b; 4, j; 5, l; 6, p; 7, g; 8, c; 9, e; 10, h; 11, k; 12, m; 13, o; 14, n; 15, i; 16, a; 17, q; 18, r.

Texas: the LA of the South?

Moviegoers, think Texas instead of California when you see your next film. Chances are, at least a portion of it was filmed in the Lone Star State.

With its geographic diversity and scenic beauty, Texas has been the filming site for more than 1,300 projects since 1910. One of the state's earliest films was a movie about two World War I fighter pilots vying for the attentions of a young woman. Titled *Wings*, it was a box-office hit in 1927. It was the only silent movie to win an Academy Award for Best Picture—and that's really saying something (without saying anything).

The Queen of Tejano Music

Born in 1971 in Lake Jackson, Selena Quintanilla was singing by the age of 3 and was with a band started by her father when she was 9. The family moved to Corpus Christi, where the young singer produced her first album, *Mis Primeras Grabaciones*. Soon she was the top singer in the Tejano music industry. In 1989, she signed with Capitol Records (Latin label) and her career, it seemed, was on its way.

She met guitarist Chris Pérez, and they married in 1992. When a fan named Yolanda Saldivar approached the family and suggested that she be the head of a new fan club for the singer, the rising star's luck seemed to be never-ending. Grammy awards followed, and in February 1995, the young Tejana performed at a sold-out concert at the Houston Astrodome. But shortly after that, the music was over.

That same year, affection turned to distrust—Yolanda was fired. In a dispute with Yolanda in March, the singer was shot and killed. Several months later, her long-cherished dream was realized by her family members when a song from her English-language album became a hit—she had crossed over into the mainstream pop-music market.

It's always a tragedy when death comes too early. But Selena Quintanilla-Pérez she lives on in her recorded music and in the hearts of her fans, who come from around the world to tour the museum in Corpus Christi established by her father.

The Vaughan Brothers: Jimmie and Stevie Ray

Mention musical icons, and Jimmie and Stevie Ray Vaughan are sure to come to anyone's mind. Their musical ability would probably never have been realized had it not been for an injury sustained by Jimmie.

Born and raised in Oak Hill (a Dallas suburb), both brothers listened to top-40 radio music (a genre that was invented in Dallas) and became hooked on the variety of musical styles and talents they heard over the airwaves. Older brother Jimmie, though, loved playing football, and until the age of 13 had never played a musical instrument . . . until fate stepped in. That year, Jimmie was injured playing football, and during his recuperation he had too much time on his hands. A friend of the family gave young Jimmie a guitar to occupy him—and the rest is history.

Jimmie started his first band, the Swinging Pendulums, when he was only 15, then joined another band, the Chessmen, when he was 16, playing Dallas nightclubs. One famous musician he opened a concert for was Jimi Hendrix.

Jimmie began to develop a love for the blues; he helped form a blues-and-soul band, Texas Storm, in 1969. The band moved to Austin, and brother Stevie Ray joined them, playing bass guitar.

Kim Wilson and Jimmie Vaughan then formed the Fabulous Thunderbirds; they became the house band for a nightclub, Antone's. When Jimmie opened for blues icon Muddy Waters, he tried imitating the bluesman's style. It is said that Waters told him afterward that he was the one to carry on the blues tradition for future generations.

Meanwhile, though Stevie Ray was just as musically gifted as his brother, he was beset by troubles ranging from alcoholism to drug addiction. Although he had played and recorded with such greats as David Bowie (on the *Let's Dance* album) and played with the band Double Trouble (which had a gold album), Stevie Ray had his demons to reckon with; he checked into rehab in 1987. This seemed to turn things around for him, and his fourth album, *In Step*, won him a Grammy.

The two brothers recorded the album *Family Style* in 1990, but just before the album's release, tragedy struck: Just after boarding a helicopter headed to Chicago, Stevie Ray Vaughan and four other passengers were killed. Today, the Stevie Ray Vaughan Memorial, a life-size statue of the artist, faces the sunset along the Town Lake Trail at Auditorium Shores.

Stevie Ray's death devastated his brother; Jimmie retreated from life until fellow musician Eric Clapton invited him to join him in performing at the Royal Albert Hall in London. Afterward, Jimmie recorded his first album, Strange Pleasure, which was dedicated to his brother; the CD was nominated for a Grammy for best blues album. Now, even though he's a huge celebrity—Steven Thomas Erlewine, editor of All Music Guide, calls him a living legend not only in Texas but throughout the United States—Jimmie Vaughan continues to play daily.

Had It Not Been for a Birthday Disappointment . . .

The boy wanted a bicycle for his birthday, and the shiny one in the front window of a hardware store in Tupelo, Mississippi, was the only one that would do. There was one obstacle, though: money. The boy's parents were a bit low on funds, and when his mother saw the price of the bike, her heart sank.

Then she spotted something else nearby—something they could afford. It was a guitar, and the price was right: $12.95. She bought the guitar and gave it to her son.

The boy must have been disappointed at first, but by and by, he began trying to play his new guitar. Then he realized that he was good—quite good—at singing and playing. Later, when he and his family moved to Memphis, he recorded his first songs at the famous Sun Studio there, as a gift for his mom.

You know the rest of this boy's story. The name Elvis Presley became a household word as his fame spread worldwide, and his larger-than-life stage persona and dance style earned him the moniker "Elvis the Pelvis."

Of course, there's more to this story, and it concerns another ambitious singer named Buddy Holly. Here it is, in a nutshell: When he was still a rising star, Elvis Presley performed one night at the Cotton Club of Lubbock, Texas. At that time, the Cotton Club was unique in that its stage was open to all performers regardless of their sex, skin color, or musical genre. Buddy Holly was one of the people who heard and saw Elvis perform at the Cotton Club. Holly's music was forever changed after that. Because of a birthday disappointment many years earlier, Elvis Presley, Buddy Holly, and the Cotton Club became major chapters in the annals of music history.

Today, the entire city of Lubbock is awash in all things related to the singer who made his songs "Peggy Sue" and "That'll Be the Day" classics, including a Buddy Holly statue and Buddy Holly Walk of Fame, the latter of which honors those Texans significant to the entertainment industry. One highlight of the tributes to the singer, who died in a plane crash in 1959 is the Buddy Holly Center, which celebrates his brief life. Also, in 2007, the center celebrated the Cotton Club with an exhibit called "Cotton Club: Halfway to Slaton," because in its early days, it was a stopping place for bands traveling between Dallas and Los Angeles.

"The Showcase of the Southwest" Makes a Comeback

In the 1930s, the town of El Paso had as one of its bragging rights the Plaza Theatre, which gave the city an opportunity to view not only film but also stage theater and musical performances. But later, the popularity of television resulted in a decline in the size of audiences in this ornate, rococo-designed theater with Spanish Colonial Revival architecture, and it was closed. Not long ago, the beautiful old theater was scheduled for demolition so a parking lot could be built in its place.

Luckily for all of us, though, the El Paso Community Foundation, with some help from famous entertainer Rita Moreno, saved it from demolition and began fundraising efforts to pay what amounted to $38 million for restoring the old theater. Now reopened and the proud owner of a newly refurbished $60,000 Wurlitzer organ, the 2,100-seat theater has recently had the likes of B.B. King performing under its dome, and Moreno herself has also performed there. The showcase of the Southwest is back.

The Live Music Capital of the World

If you can't find your favorite style of music played on any of hundreds of stages in Austin—from reggae, pop, blues, and country to swing, jazz, and rock—then you're not looking hard enough.

Austin is also home to the long-running PBS special *Austin City Limits*. Broadcast continually since 1976, the music special is the longest-running show ever on the PBS channel. Although the free passes to shows are virtually impossible to obtain, you can take in a free guided tour of the studio every Friday.

"Pretty Women Don't Need Money"

One day Roy Orbison's wife, Claudette, was about to go shopping. Orbison had just written a song especially for her and was discussing just what to name it with his friend Bill Dees. As Claudette was leaving, Roy asked her if she needed money.

Dees looked at Roy and quipped, "Don't you know that pretty women don't need money?" Orbison and Dees looked at each other and said in unison, "Pretty Woman!" It was the perfect title for Orbison's tribute to his wife, and the song continues to enjoy enduring popularity—it was most recently used as the title song for the movie Pretty Woman, starring Julia Roberts and Richard Gere.

Roy Orbison in 1960 without his trademark sunglasses, with his fan, David Coffield. Courtesy David Coffield, Jacksonville, Florida.

Orbison grew up in the town of Wink, Texas, and the Roy Orbison Museum there has a collection of all sorts of memorabilia related to the famous musician. Of all the songs he ever wrote, "Pretty Woman" is perhaps the most famous. Good thing Claudette decided to go shopping that day—she helped make her husband's song, and Wink, famous.

Redheaded Stranger: Musical Renaissance Man

Born in Abbott, Texas, in 1933, Willie Nelson began playing a guitar when he was only 4 years old. He divided his time between Tennessee and Texas, trying to sell his lyrics for tunes, before he hit on the idea of performing what he wrote. "Red-Headed Stranger" was a hit in 1975, and his career took off.

Nelson has acted too, doing equally well on television and on-screen. Besides all this, though, he hasn't forgotten the common person: He has a philanthropic bent, devoting his energies to Farm Aid (which gives assistance to farmers) and supports the greening of America by pushing biofuel into the forefront of energy technology.

Despite his extreme popularity, though, Nelson has remained an approachable, friendly guy: Meeting him once behind Tootsie's Orchid Lounge in Nashville, I found him to be as genuine and humble as any person on the street—no stranger, redheaded or otherwise, to anyone.

Q & A

Q. Where is the real Southfork Ranch that was used for the filming of the TV series Dallas?

A. Plano, Texas. There are guided tours—and, yes, you can even see the gun that shot J.R. Ewing.

Q. What singing cowboy made the boll weevil famous in a song about the bane of the Texas cotton farmer?

A. Tex Ritter.

Q. What town is the site of Resistol-brand hat factory, owned by Hatco, Inc., that provided the hats for the character J.R. Ewing on the long-running television show, Dallas?

A. Garland.

Q. What did Texas's 73rd Legislature name "Texas Official Opera House"?

A. The Grand 1894 Opera House, in Galveston.

Q. In the Central Texas Wing of the Commemorative Air Force in San Marcos is a replica of a Japanese torpedo bomber. In what movie was this bomber used?

A. The movie Tora! Tora! Tora! starring Martin Balsam.

Q. What museum in Jefferson might be the delight of Gone With the Wind buffs?

A. Scarlett O'Hardy's Gone With the Wind Museum, which contains one of the largest collections of Gone With the Wind memorabilia anywhere.

Q. What musician who became famous for his "Maple Leaf Rag" tune was born in Texarkana and still holds the title "King of Ragtime"?

A. Scott Joplin. You may best remember his music as the sound track for the movie The Sting, which starred Paul Newman and Robert Redford.

Q. What entertainment venue in Arlington has been voted best live country music show by the Country Music Association for at least the last five years in a row?

A. Johnnie High's Country Music Revue.

Q. What city celebrates Red Steagall's musical heritage with an event held every October?

A. Fort Worth, which celebrates the Red Steagall Cowboy Gathering and Western Swing Festival.

Q. What town was the site of the film Michael, starring John Travolta, as the bad-boy angel?

A. La Grange.

Q. What bank in the town of Pilot Point was the site of filming for the movie Bonnie and Clyde?

A. The Farmers & Merchants Bank Building.

Q. What long-playing rock group bills themselves as "That Little Ol' Band from Texas"?

A. ZZ Top.

FLORA, FAUNA, AND NATURAL PHENOMENA

The Great Camel Experiment

This story has bits of history going back to 1836, through the Civil War; it also has to do with transportation, entertainment, entrepreneurial endeavors . . . and, of course, camels.

It began in 1836, when Major George Crosman recommended that camels be used in the arid West in the U.S. Army's efforts to subdue Native Americans there. The so-called Shield Amendment to appropriate the funds to purchase the camels was finally passed in 1855. The first shipment of 33 camels arrived at Indianola, Texas, in 1856, and finally arrived at Camp Verde, northwest of San Antonio.

One of the initial camel treks was made to the Big Bend Country. The first reports were favorable for these beasts that history has called ships of the desert: They can carry as much as 600 pounds of supplies easily and travel not just dozens but hundreds of miles before needing water—and they eat virtually anything. Another shipment of camels was ordered, and 41 more were delivered to Camp Verde.

Most of these animals were used to transport soldiers and supplies in the surveying of Texas prairie; they also were employed as beasts of burden during the Civil War. Many camels passed into Confederate hands and were used to transport Southern gold—cotton—to Mexico for supplies and to obtain funds for the Southern cause.

As time passed, the army's infatuation with camels became displeasure: They stank, they spit, they frightened horses and other livestock—and in the modern vernacular, they had an attitude. Anyone who has ever ridden a camel knows what this means.

Fast-forward to more modern days. In 1995, the Texas Camel Corps, based in Valley Mills, came into existence. Created by owner Doug Baum, the purpose of the corps is to educate the public, empower at-risk youth, and make history come alive.

In 1999, the corps began offering camel treks to the public, taking people on the same historic trail through Big Bend Country that the original camels trod in the 1850s and 1960s (and also have treks in Egypt as well). They also offer programs for at-risk youth, trying to have a positive impact on young lives by having the youth work with the camels on treks called CamelQuests.

The corps' animals have also been used in movies (they're listed with the Texas Film Commission), and Christmastime finds the camels busy, traveling the state in recreations of the Christmas miracle. Check out their Web site (see the "Virtual Texas" section near the back of this book).

DID YOU KNOW?

Shell Game

Did you know that the shell called a lightning whelk is the official state shell of Texas?

Sweetwater Snakes

Years ago, the ranchers in the area of Sweetwater were plagued with an overabundance of rattlesnakes. They began having organized gatherings to eradicate the venomous snakes, and now Sweetwater lays claim to what has become the biggest rattlesnake roundup on the globe.

Events at the World's Largest Rattlesnake Roundup, which is held every March, include displays of thousands of live rattlesnakes, fried rattlesnake for hungry visitors, and a beauty contest in which Miss Snake Charmer gets her choice of milking or skinning a rattlesnake, as part of the competition.

. . . And While We're Slinking Around the Subject

Every year around St. Patrick's Day, the World Championship Rattlesnake Races are held in San Patricio. They started this in 1972, but don't worry, the snakes race in enclosed lanes, so you're relatively safe from being bitten. You can also enjoy some fried rattlesnake while you're there.

A Different Kind of Dog Tale

In Lubbock, you can get up close and personal with a different kind of dog. It is here that one of the last prairie dog towns in the nation still exists. In the early days of Texas, these animals were the bane of ranchers' existence, but now Lubbock embraces them, protecting them in a 248-acre village called Prairie Dog Town.

Always a Starry Night in Big Bend Country

In 1932, an amateur astronomer named William J. McDonald dreamed of having an observatory in Big Bend Country. On the peak of Mount Locke (just west of Fort Davis), an observatory was finally built at this high elevation (6,790-plus feet). The realization of McDonald's dream was due to the combined efforts of the University of Texas at Austin, Pennsylvania State University, two German universities, and Stanford University. The telescope they have on the premises is among the largest in the world, and visitors book an opportunity, usually months in advance, to see the stars and planets through the observatory's 107-inch telescope.

Are the stars out tonight? They are if you're at the McDonald Observatory.

The Scaly Displaced Are Honored Here

Long ago, alligators called the area now known as San Jacinto Plaza, El Paso, home. They're no longer part of this downtown area, but a sculptor by the name of Luis Jiménez has honored them in a fiberglass work of art called Plaza de los Lagartos, which you can see when you visit the plaza in the heart of (gatorless) downtown El Paso.

A Sheepish Tale

Not only is the area known as Edwards Plateau, in west central Texas, the top sheep-growing area in the United States but also more wool comes from the entire state of Texas than from any other state in the United States.

Tribute in Muleshoe

Northwest of Lubbock, the town of Muleshoe has a statue of a mule, which stands at Main Street and U.S. Highway 84. The townsfolk figured because their town was named Muleshoe and because mules carted early settlers to the area and then helped plow the land, they ought to honor the animal.

The National Mule Memorial—they call it the world's largest muleshoe—is 22 feet tall and 17 feet wide and made of fiberglass. It seems to just beg passersby to stop and have their picture made next to it—and a lot of them do.

This Couple Has Green Thumbs!

Northwest of Fort Worth, slightly north of Mineral Wells and Weatherford, is an amazing array of acres of flowers, sculptures, and breathtaking beauty. It started in 1972, when Billie Clark had her private garden here. Her love for all things bright and beautiful led her and her husband, Max, to create a foundation and donate land for the purpose of aesthetics and education here; they opened the Clark Gardens Botanical Park in April 2000.

The landscape is embellished with many plants and shrubs indigenous to Texas, and some plants have been made what the gardens' Web site refers to as "Texas-adaptable." The high point of the year at the gardens is the last week in April, when more than 1,200 varieties of irises are on display.

All "Fur" a Good Cause

When Hurricane Katrina struck New Orleans in 2005, many evacuees were obliged to leave their beloved pets behind. Of course, you probably remember that these evacuees eventually arrived in Houston, to take refuge in the Astrodome.

The city of Houston has a heart as big as Texas itself. Realizing that many of the evacuees were pet owners, the members of the Houston Society for the Prevention of Cruelty to Animals (SPCA) served as coordinators of the rescue efforts for the pets in New Orleans and shipped the animals to be reunited with their owners.

Alice Sarmiento wrote, in the Houston SPCA newsletter, about her memories of the hurricane, recalling that within 12 hours of the call for help from the Louisiana Society for the Prevention of Cruelty to Animals, the Houston SPCA took in more than 260 animals, seeking shelter for them until they could be returned to their owners.

They took in not only animals from Louisiana, she wrote, but also "accepted almost 600 animals from evacuees of the Houston Astrodome" itself, and "provided free temporary board, shelter, and care to the pets" of those affected by the hurricane.

This rescue and reunion was so amazing, it was documented in an *Animal Planet* special entitled *Animal Planet Heroes: Hurricane Rescues,* which aired that same year. This kind of achievement on behalf of furry friends is nothing new to Houston: A local TV program entitled *Animal Cops: Houston,* which deals with animal cruelty cases and rescues, received the Genesis Award in 2005 in the reality program category.

"I Dare You" and Weather History

It was July 27, 1943, and a "surprise" hurricane was in the Gulf of Mexico. It was called a surprise then because, owing to censorship issues of World War II and the concern about U-boats threatening the Gulf Coast, radio communication from ships (even those that might include reports of storms) was hushed. And this was before satellite imagery and the *Weather Channel* as well—so coastal Texas was caught off guard.

As they played a game of poker, a handful of pilots at Bryan Army Air Base (Bryan, Texas) were observing the weather as it approached land. Some of the pilots were British, and the talk turned to some of their most daring flights. They dared an American pilot, flight instructor Colonel Joe Duckworth, to fly into the hurricane—saying that his trainer-plane was too small and that flying into such a storm had never been done before.

He took their dare: He flew his North American AT-6 trainer directly into the hurricane. He did it not once but twice—the second time, he took the air base's weather official with him.

Duckworth is now known as history's first "hurricane hunter," and on July 27, 2007, he was acknowledged on the Weather Channel for his bravery. The air force will always remember Duckworth for saving pilots' lives by teaching them to fly using modern instruments (and he has been called the father of modern-day air force instrument flying). The National Oceanic and Atmospheric Administration will always remember him for inspiring weather forecasters to be a part of the weather rather than to simply observe it, and because of this, he has saved thousands of lives that might have been lost due to hurricanes and other severe weather.

Col. Joe B. Duckworth, the first hurricane hunter. Reprinted by permission from *Air Force Magazine*, published by the Air Force Association.

Sonora, Where You Can See a Butterfly . . . in a Cave!

The town of Sonora (in Hill Country) has a kind of gem just west of town, in the nature of a cave unlike any other. Called the Caverns of Sonora, the cave is unusual in that it is still growing. Only 10 percent of the caves in the world are still growing, or developing, as this one is.

Further, the ceilings, walls, and floors bloom in a profusion of color that you won't see anywhere else, in such beautiful formations the National Speleological Society has called impossible. Yet they are here, for you to see and tour.

One of the most amazing sights on the cave tour is a huge butterfly created totally by a mineral formation that emerges from the ceiling. The butterfly, with its cream-colored wings outstretched as if it's about to take flight, is even used as the cave's logo.

In November 2006, a malicious tourist snapped off a portion of the butterfly's wing. Although the butterfly is still a beautiful and awe-inspiring thing to behold, the docents tell me that this was like "stealing a national treasure." They also tell me that if the piece of the wing is returned, the butterfly can be repaired. . . .

This mineral "butterfly" literally grew out of the walls. Courtesy Caverns of Sonora/Gary Bedreaux.

A Matching Game

See if you can match the description with the place, group, or animal name. If you're a Texan, these should be easy (answers below, but don't peek!).

1. Official state large mammal
2. Only natural body of water in the state
3. Approximately 16 million
4. Official state small mammal
5. Has more species of birds than any other area in North America
6. Recently reintroduced into Big Bend Country
7. First commercially cloned horse in America
8. Bluebonnet capital of Texas

a. Caddo Lake
b. Brazoria County
c. Armadillo
d. Cattle population
e. Longhorn
f. Royal Blue Boon Too
g. Desert bighorn sheep
h. Burnet

Answers: 1, e; 2 a; 3, d; 4, c; 5, b; 6, g; 7, f; 8, h.

Brighter Days, Where the Price of Admission Is a Bag of . . . Carrots?

Approximately 40 miles from San Antonio, you can visit some of our favorite mammals on Earth at Brighter Days Horse Refuge, a nonprofit center for abused and injured horses. Established by Jeannie and Bill Weatherholtz, the rehabilitation refuge has taken in dozens of horses rescued from cruelty and abandonment cases, as well as race horses too old for the track. Brighter Days has both sponsorship and adoption programs but welcomes visitors to come see and pet the horses that would have died under horrific circumstances had it not been for the refuge. There are approximately 65 horses currently in the care of the refuge, so you won't lack for horses to pet and hang around with. The price is admission is only the cost of a bag of carrots and apples, but they take green donations—the kind with pictures of presidents on them—as well.

This is place does give horses whose days were numbered a better life, as you can see in the "Happy Endings" section of the refuge's Web site (see the "Virtual Texas" section near the back of this book). When you come visit, be prepared: along with your bag of apples and carrots, bring along a horse trailer—just in case.

Holy Toledo! It's Bat Time!

Austin boasts one of the world's largest city-dwelling colonies of Mexican free-tailed bats. They make their home under the Congress Avenue Bridge, and every sunset between April to October, they leave their concrete home in a spectacle that darkens the skies as they head out for a dinner of mosquitoes.

The bats have become so much a part of the Austin experience that the city created a bat statue near the bridge, there is a bat hotline, the minor-league hockey club is named the Austin Ice Bats, and the city library has a bat as a mascot (who is named Echo) that they use for children's programs.

Austin is also home to Bat Conservation International, or BCI (see the "Virtual Texas" section near the back of this book), an organization that is working to change the negative perception people have of bats.

Another Bat Story: Bracken Bat Cave and Nature Reserve

Just outside San Antonio is a priceless natural resource that BCI hopes will help educate people around the globe about the true nature of bats: the Bracken Bat Cave and Nature Reserve. This isn't just any bat cave: Bracken is home to the world's largest bat colony, and probably its oldest; scientists theorize that bats have been making this cavern their home for more than 10,000 years. Recently BCI purchased more than 690 acres of land surrounding the cave, saving it from development, as San Antonio's borders have grown ever closer.

The people of San Antonio should count their blessings for having these winged creatures as their neighbors, for in one single summer night, the bat colony can consume an average of 200 tons of mosquitoes and other flying pests—and remember, mosquitoes carry diseases such as West Nile virus and are capable of damaging valuable crops.

Although the cave is open only to BCI members on select nights, interested bat friends can view video clips of the bats as they emerge from the cave at night. Also, BCI hopes to open an interpretive center soon, to educate people about the good that bats do for our world.

A Sticky Subject

Because so much of Texas is arid, it stands to reason that Texans celebrate a plant common to deserts: the lowly cactus. This holds true especially for the town of Sanderson (population nearly 900), which calls itself the "Cactus Capital of Texas".

And, because all Texans seem to have a penchant for celebrating virtually everything, Sanderson holds an annual Prickly Pear Pachanga on Columbus Day weekend. Pachanga means "party" in Spanish, something that Texans know how to do in more than one language.

See the next chapter for a recipe on how to cook prickly pear, courtesy of Terrell County Visitors Center in Sanderson.

Raylene, the Cactus Queen. The story goes that this girl, a beauty contestant in the 1940s, wanted so badly to win, she made a swimsuit entirely out of cacti. Courtesy Sanderson Community Development Association.

Strange But True!

Sad Tree

In DeLeon, Texas, they have an unusual tree that has been mentioned in *Ripley's Believe It Or Not!* This tree is called a weeping oak because its great branches *grow downward.*

They Celebrate Everything in Texas . . .

As I've mentioned, Texans celebrate absolutely everything, including the lowly, sometimes pain-inducing fire ant. The town of Marshall has an annual Fire Ant Festival every October. I never could discern if that's because they have more fire ants than any other place in the state or just because they needed something to celebrate in the fall.

On a similar note, the town of Cooper holds its Chiggerfest every October. You might get a burning itch to attend one or both of these celebrations.

DID YOU KNOW?

Bird Boon

One of the jewels of Texas is the Sabal Palm Audubon Sanctuary in Brownsville. Hailed as one of the most enchanting naturally occurring ecosystems in the state, this 557-acre paradise is sanctuary to many endangered species, including the buff-bellied hummingbird, a variety of other migrating birds, and the ocelot, among others. According to a marine biologist friend of mine, the Sabal Palm Audubon Sanctuary is called a "critical ecosystem" because of the amazing water-filtration job it performs for the region. The sanctuary is open for tours daily except on New Year's Day, Christmas Day, and Thanksgiving.

Sacred Rocks

In Llano (north of San Antonio), Enchanted Rock State Natural Area has an old history with Native American peoples. It was revered by some as having ghosts, because expansion and contraction (with the changing temperatures) of the great rock cause it to creak and moan. Legend has it that one Spanish conquistador was captured by a group of Tonkawa Indians, and he eluded them by going to the rock, which swallowed him up. His captors apparently were afraid to follow him over the great rock, which legend also holds to be the site of ancient human sacrifices.

The area is open for limited tourism, so when you go, keep your wits about you!

Plants Make Ropes and Beetle Juice Makes Dyes!

In the southern and western parts of Texas grows the lechuguilla plant (botanical name: Aguve lechuguilla), the fibers of which native people in the area discovered are quite useful.

The plant, which resembles an aloe vera, is related not to the cactus but is in the lily family. Its name means "little lettuce," and it is believed that ancient aboriginal peoples use it as a food and for other purposes.

The plant grows in groups, and the spiky leaves have thorny, saw-like edges, with a needlelike tip on the end. Indigenous peoples would remove the plant's outer skin (while leaving the needle end intact), take out the fibrous inside of the plant, and pound it to separate the fiber from the skin. Using the needlelike tip, they would sew, using the fibers as a kind of thread. There were other uses for the fiber, which very much resembled regular rope fiber; people would weave it to make baskets and other kinds of containers, sandals, and rope.

The beetles (known more commonly as cochineal bugs; biological name, *Dactylopius confusus*) that are drawn to the lechuguilla are used to make a kind of natural dye. The tiny beetles (about a dozen can fit on the side of a penny) commonly make their nests, or web, on cactus such as the lechuguilla; the nests resemble small cotton bolls. Native people would remove the beetles from the cactus and crush the insects. The "juice" was initially red but after a few days would change to black, and the dye was used to stain fibers such as fabric, feathers, and even wooden items.

Next time you need to go to the hardware store for dye and rope—be thankful that you don't have to get them the hard way from the desert instead.

<u>Q & A</u>

Q. Trick question: what is the name of the cave in Boerne?

A. There isn't one. Townspeople decided that the beauty of the cave defied description, so it's simply the cave without a name.

Q. What is unique about Wonder World Cave in San Marcos?

A. Unlike every other cave in the world—which has been formed by water—Wonder World Cave was formed by an earthquake! You can touch its walls, and lights from camera flashes don't affect it as they do water-formed caves.

Q. What town in Texas has the nation's largest concentration of sandhill cranes?

A. Muleshoe. The cranes winter over there.

Q. For what stone is Texas famous (hint: one sought-after type is known as the "red plume")?

A. The agate.

Q. What place in Big Bend Country will let you mine for these stones?

A. The 3,000-acre Woodward Agate Ranch in Alpine.

Q. Speaking of Big Bend Country: Big Bend National Park has been recognized as having more species of what animal than any other national park?

A. Birds. Inside the park's boundaries, naturalists have identified more than 450 species of birds -- a national park record.

Q. What city is famous as the "aloe vera capital of the nation"?

A. Harlingen. It's home to the Forever Aloe Plantations, which hosts exhibits, gives tours, and has a gift shop.

Q. What zoological park in Texas is world famous, and why?

A. The Gladys Porter Zoo in Brownsville, because nearly all its 360-plus species of animals are in free, open exhibits (and 43 of those species are endangered)

Q. What "forest" in Monahans Sandhills State Park is not apparent to the casual observer?

A. The 40,000-acre stretch of Harvard oaks, which grow up to only 3 feet in height (their real growth is belowground, where their root system may go down as far as 90 feet, to help them survive in the desert).

Q. What city is known as the official hippo capital of Texas?

A. The town of Hutto, in the Hill Country. The city's mascot is the hippo, and as a result, there are more than 150 hippo statues across Hutto, the largest one being Henrietta the Hippo, a statue weighing in at 14,000 pounds.

Q. What fruit is grown in Pecos and is described by the Office of the Governor, Economic Development & Tourism as on a par with "Maine lobsters, French wines, and Swiss cheese"?

A. The cantaloupe, which is grown in irrigated fields and has a taste unequaled by cantaloupe grown anywhere else in the world (try it!)

Q. What is the highest point in Texas, and where is it?

A. Guadalupe Peak, elevation 8,749 feet, in Pine Springs, West Texas.

Q. What record was broken by bird-watchers in Surfside Beach in 1973?

A. In Surfside Beach, part of what is known as the Brazosport area, bird-watchers broke the national record of sighting bird species—226 species total—in their area that year.

Q. What city on the coast is known as a bird lover's paradise because it is situated at the convergence of two major flyways?

A. Harlingen.

Q. What area on the coast is famed as the principal wintering grounds for the whooping crane, a once nearly extinct species of bird?

A. The Rockport–Fulton area

Q. Who is known as the "Bird Lady of Texas" because of

her ornithological observations and research?

A. Rockport's Connie Hagar. The Connie Hagar Cottage Sanctuary, a great place for lovers of birds and nature, is open as a tourist attraction.

Q. What is the name of the vertical cavern, with an opening of approximately 40 feet and a vertical drop of approximately 140 feet, in Rocksprings, Texas?

A. Devil's Sinkhole. Designated as a State Natural Area, it is open for guided tours.

Q. Who was named by the Texas Legislature as Texas's "Ambassadors on Horseback"?

A. The Santa Rosa Palomino Club—a precision equestrian riding organization—in Vernon

Q. What city calls itself the "City of Live Oaks"?

A. Columbus, Texas. It was under the branches of one of the huge oaks there that the first court of the Third Judicial District of the Texas Republic met in 1837.

FOOD AND FASCINATING CULTURAL TIDBITS

The Official State Song (Now You Can Sing Along!)

The official state song of Texas is not "The Yellow Rose of Texas" or even "The Eyes of Texas" (the latter is the song of the University of Texas).

The music to "Texas, Our Texas" was written by Fort Worth resident William J. Marsh, and the lyrics were composed by Marsh and Gladys Yoakum Wright. It was adopted as the official state song by the legislature in 1929. Most people don't know the words, so here they are:

"Texas, Our Texas"

Texas, our Texas! All hail the mighty state!
Texas, our Texas! So wonderful, so great!
Boldest and grandest,
withstanding ev'ry test,
O Empire wide and glorious,
you stand supremely blest.

(chorus)

Texas, O Texas! Your freeborn single star,
Sends out its radiance to
nations near and far,
Emblem of freedom! It sets
our hearts aglow,
With thoughts of San Jacinto
and glorious Alamo.

(chorus)

Texas, dear Texas! From
tyrant grip now free,
Shines forth in splendor,
your star of destiny!
Mother of heroes, we come
your children true,
Proclaiming our allegiance,
our faith, our love for you.

(chorus)

Chorus:

God bless you, Texas! And keep
you brave and strong,
That you may grow in power and
worth, throughout the ages long.
God bless you, Texas! And keep
you brave and strong,
That you may grow in power and
worth, throughout the ages long.

A Taste of Texas: The Big Three

Austin resident and food aficionado Jacci Howard Bear is an expert on many things, not the least of which are foods that are Texas specialties. In one of her columns, she writes that Texas considers many foods to be its specialties, but the so-called Big Three are barbecue, chicken-fried steak, and chili (the latter of which was named the state dish of Texas by the 1977 Texas Legislature). Here's a taste of each, the recipes compliments of my godmother, Laredo resident Alice Romero.

Barbecue

Texas cattle country and the Johnson administration are said to have inspired what is now Texas-style barbecue. President Lyndon B. Johnson and his wife, Lady

Bird Johnson, hosted Texas-style cookouts at the White House during his administration, and the rest is culinary history: Texas and barbecue are now synonymous.

My daddy was famous for his barbecue, cooked cowboy-style over an open pit using direct heat. Like him, George Cooper of Llano, Texas, uses this same approach at his restaurant, Cooper's Old Time Pit Bar-B-Que, located in Llano. His place is deservedly famous for its sausages, beef brisket, and even goat.

Because of the influx of so many European immigrants into Texas—most notably German and Czech—they brought their own style of cooking with them, and it has been blended into the Texas culinary mix. They are said to have had the practice of taking leftover cuts of meats and sausages and putting them on the grill, using a variety of seasonings. One taste of Texas barbecue, regardless of where it's cooked and what method is used, will have you saying, "Hey, y'all, this is good!"

Classic Barbecue Sauce

Use for whatever meat you choose.

1 medium onion, diced

3 cloves garlic, minced

½ cup vinegar (many cooks prefer apple cider vinegar)

½ cup Worcestershire sauce

1 jalapeño pepper, seeded and diced, or 2 crushed red peppers

2 tablespoons prepared mustard

½ cup molasses or ½ cup packed brown sugar

2 cups ketchup

1 cup water

Salt, to taste

Directions: Combine all ingredients and simmer in an uncovered pot for at least 30 minutes.

Chicken-Fried Steak

Yield: 4 servings

I have used this recipe with equal success with pheasant, venison, dove, and rabbit. If you have a Dutch oven, you can simmer the dish, covered, for about an hour on top of the stove instead of baking it.

> 2 pounds top round steak
> Meat tenderizer
> 1 cup flour (many cooks prefer unbleached, all-purpose flour)
> 2 cups beef broth
> Salt, pepper, and garlic powder, to taste

Directions: Tenderize steak by sprinkling meat tenderizer on both sides of meat, using fork to penetrate meat. Dredge steaks with flour and flash-fry in hot oil on top of stove till browned on both sides. Preheat oven to 350 degrees Fahrenheit.

Placed flash-fried steaks in a baking dish (recommended size is 13" × 9" × 3"). Prepare thin gravy by adding 3 tablespoons of flour to the drippings in the frying pan; add a little more oil if you need to. When gravy is brown, add beef broth, salt, pepper, and garlic powder. Stir constantly until smooth and bubbling.

When the gravy is thickened, pour it over steaks. Put baking pan in oven and bake, covered, for 35 minutes. Serve with rice or mashed potatoes.

Chili, or, In Texas, It's Always Chili, Even in Winter

Chili is probably the most often cooked dish in the entire Lone Star State, but there's one town that has a true reverence and passion, even obsession, for it. The population of the city of Terlingua, which is normally about

250, swells to 5,000 every first Saturday in November when the town holds the annual Terlingua International Chili Championship. The chili aficionados are referred to as "chiliheads," and the first chiliheads were a couple of humorists named H. Allen Smith and Wick Fowler, who began in 1967 what is now a beloved, heated contest.

Texas-Style Chili

Yield: 8 to 10 servings

2 pounds ground round
1 large onion, finely chopped
2 jalapeño peppers, seeded and chopped
2 cloves garlic, minced
2 tablespoons chili powder
2 teaspoons cumin
1 teaspoon salt
1 can (12 ounces) tomato paste
2 cups water
1 can (15 ounces) pinto beans, rinsed and drained

Directions: Crumble meat in large pot with all other ingredients except water, tomato paste, and beans. Cook until slightly brown; you may wish to drain off excess fat. When meat is brown, add tomato paste and water; simmer about 1½ hours. Add beans and simmer another ½ hour. Add more hot pepper if desired.

A Globe by Any Other Name Could Only Be . . . in Texas

Sorry for the joke, but Shakespeare liked to make them too, so it just can't be helped, but even in Texas, you can find vestiges of the bard and his famous theater. On the grounds of Odessa College you will find a replica of not only the Globe Theatre but also Anne Hathaway's house (the bard's wife) as they appeared in London and Stratford-upon-Avon, respectively. The theater offers entertainment of all types, including, of course, an annual Shakespeare festival the last week in August and the first week in September.

Strange But True!

Wichita Falls—Again!

The city of Wichita Falls was originally named after the Wichita Indians and a waterfall that, until 1886, made the town famous. In that year, a flood struck the town—and the waterfall was washed away. A re-creation of this waterfall has been constructed by townspeople and business owners. Completed in 1987, the new falls is about a mile from the Convention & Visitors Bureau and faces north on Interstate 44 and is 54 feet high, recirculating water at the rate of 3,500 gallons a minute.

The Other Stonehenge

Stonehenge II in Texas. Sydney Hill and her dog, Baby, posed for this shot. Courtesy Doug and Shaleah Hill.

In Hunt, Texas (slightly northeast of San Antonio), you can see a replica of England's Stonehenge. It all started when a man named Doug Hill had been doing some construction and had one large stone left over. His neighbor, Al Shepperd, saw the stone in the field near Hill's house and brought him a copy of an article about Stonehenge, asking him to recreate it in the field. Inspired, Hill began construction, using hollow plaster instead of the original solid stone, and after nearly five months, the site now referred to as Stonehenge II was finished. It is now flanked with two re-created figures from statues on Easter Island.

Easter Island statues grace the area around Stonehenge II as well. Courtesy Doug and Shaleah Hill.

Stonehenge II is open to the public, and donations are accepted.

DID YOU KNOW?

If You Can't Pronounce It, Rename It

If you leave Austin and drive northwest for about 45 minutes, you'll come to the town of Oatmeal.

According to Texas Escapes (an online magazine), the town was named after a German businessman named Othneil. After a while, people just started saying "Oatmeal," and the name stuck like, well, cooked oatmeal.

Some years back, when the town of Oatmeal came across hard times and was in danger of disappearing, the townsfolk decided to capitalize on their town's name. They came up with the annual Oatmeal Festival, held every Labor Day weekend. To advertise the Oatmeal Festival, the townsfolk painted their water tower to look like a red-and-gold box of three-minute Quaker Oats.

Massive Museum

The city of Canyon, Texas (in the Panhandle) is home to the largest history museum in the state. The Panhandle-Plains Historical Museum, measuring 285,000 square feet, contains so many exhibits relating to Texas history and its peoples that it's said that you can virtually traverse the area of Texas—26,000 square miles—in one day by touring this museum.

Bring your walking shoes!

Uncertain and Its Certain History

The town of Uncertain got its name because it was located near Uncertain Landing, which was given the moniker by steamboat captains who were uncertain as how to securely moor their vessels.

Hot Topic

The diminutive pepper with the big bang—the jalapeño—was discovered growing in the Americas by that navigation-challenged explorer, Christopher Columbus. Upon bringing it to Europe, Columbus's hot discovery was named Calcutta pepper by a German botanist—after all, everyone, including Columbus, believed that the explorer had made landfall in India.

Hundreds of years later, the 74th Legislature in Texas named the powerful little chili the state's official pepper.

Town Names, Then and Now

I came across perhaps a hundred towns whose names had changed at least once since their founding. Here is just a sampling. Cover up the new names of the cities and towns and see if you can guess what names replaced the old town names:

Old Name(s)	New Name
Barbers Hill	Mont Belvieu
Buck Snort	Buena Vista
Burleson	Lampasas
Clute's Place	Clute
Díaz	San Benito
Earpville, Steal Easy	Longview
Encina	Uvalde
Fillmore	Plano
Gouldsboro	Talco
Highlands	La Marque
Mark Belt	Pearland
Martin's Gap	Fairy
Patton	Crystal Beach
Prairie View	Bridge City

Running Brushy	Cedar Park
Shoal Point	Texas City
Stryker	Pluck
Taylorsville	Taylor
Turkey Creek, Schleicher	Cross Plains
Twist	Dalhart
Washington-on-the-Brazos	Washington
Winkler	Wink

I Hope You're Hungry! Here Are More Recipes

Perhaps nowhere else in the country can you get some Mexican food as good as Texans make it—as a matter of fact, this fusion of cultures and flavors has its own name—Tex-Mex.

To get you started on your own Tex-Mex cooking adventure, here's a fantastic tamale recipe from Austin resident Esther Zubiate. Cooking it myself, smelling the masa harina as I mixed it, had me going down memory lane, to a time when my godmother taught me and my mom how to make these delicacies:

Esther Zubiate's Homemade Beef Tamales

Yield: 36 tamales

I save the garlic and use it later in the recipe, rather than discarding it. Also, I tried a solid shortening instead of lard, and that works (though nothing tastes as good as lard in this recipe). I also didn't tie my husks, just packed them closely in the steamer basket. This recipe is very involved and time-consuming, but while you're doing it, gather the family around and have some sharing time. It will become one of your most treasured memories.

4½ pounds boneless chuck roast

4 cloves garlic

Cold water

3 packages (8 ounces each) dried corn husks

4 dried ancho chiles

2½ tablespoons vegetable oil

2½ tablespoons all-purpose flour

1 cup beef broth

1 teaspoon each of cumin seed and ground cumin

2 cloves garlic, minced

2 teaspoons chopped fresh oregano

1 teaspoon red pepper flakes

1 teaspoon white vinegar

Salt and pepper, to taste

3 cups lard

9 cups masa harina

Directions: Put beef and cloves garlic in a big pot. Cover it with cold water and bring to a boil over very high heat. As soon as the water is boiling, reduce heat to simmer and cover pot. Let simmer for 3½ hours, until beef is tender and shreds easily. When the beef is done, remove if from the pot. Reserve 5 cups cooking liquid and discard garlic cloves. Let the meat cool slightly, then finely shred it with a fork.

Place corn husks in a large container and cover with warm water. Let them soak for hours until soft and pliable. You may need to weigh them down with an inverted plate or heavy can.

Toast the ancho chiles in a cast-iron skillet, making sure not to burn them. Let them cook, then remove stems and seeds. Crumble and grind them in a clean coffee grinder or with a mortar and pestle.

Heat oil in a large, heavy skillet. Mix in flour and allow to brown slightly. Pour in 1 cup of the reserved beef broth and stir until smooth. Mix in ground chiles, cumin seeds and ground cumin, minced garlic, oregano, red pepper flakes, vinegar, and salt and pepper. Stir shredded beef into skillet and cover. Let simmer all together for 45 minutes.

Place lard and salt in a large mixing bowl. Whip with an electric mixer on high speed until it's fluffy. Add the masa harina and beat at low speed until well mixed. Pour in the reserved cooking liquid a little at a time, until the mixture is the consistency of soft cookie dough.

Drain water from corn husks. Flatten out each husk, one at a time, with the narrow end facing you, and spread approximately 2 tablespoons of the masa mixture onto the top 2/3 of the husk. Spread about 1 tablespoon of the meat mixture down the middle of the masa mixture. Roll up the corn husk, starting at the long side. Fold the narrow end of the husk onto the rolled tamale and tie it with a piece of butcher's twine. Repeat this process with each husk.

Place tamales in a steamer basket. Steam over boiling water for approximately 1 hour, until the masa mixture is firm and holds its shape. Make sure that you don't run out of water and therefore out of steam. Serve immediately, allowing each person to unwrap his or her own tamales. Allow any leftovers (still in husks) to cool, uncovered, then cover and refrigerate.

"Cactus Capital Of Texas" Seven-Layer Cactus Dip

This recipe was given to me by Hazel Gully of Sanderson, Texas. Because the town is the cactus capital of Texas, it seemed only appropriate for her to share a recipe using cactus.

Miss Hazel, as I call her, wanted me to impart this information to those of you who aren't familiar with cactus: Nopalitas are the small pads of the cactus, and the prickly pear cactus is also known as nopal to Texans. Prickly pear cacti are found virtually everywhere in the Lone Star State—and there are approximately 3,000 varieties of nopal, Miss Hazel says.

"The ones [cactus] you eat have small glochids, which are the little areas where the stickers are," she wrote me once, "and nopalita is the name for the smaller pads, which do not have full-grown glochids, so they're easier to handle and prepare for cooking."

She also told me that when these glochids are sliced and sautéed, they taste a bit like a slimy green bean, and people often cut the bitter taste with lime juice.

At any rate, here's the recipe she shared with me. It makes a regular appearance at the Prickly Pear Pachanga held in Sanderson each Columbus Day weekend.

2 avocados

2 tablespoons lemon juice

1 can refried beans or 1 cup mashed beans

Water or ketchup, as needed

1 cup cooked ground meat, well drained

1 cup chopped, boiled, or canned nopalitos

1 carton (12 ounces) sour cream

1 cup mixed, grated Colby and Monterrey Jack cheese

½ cup sliced black olives

1 tomato, chopped fine

Garlic, salt, and pepper, to taste

Directions: Peel and mash avocados and add lemon juice to retain color. If needed, add a little ketchup or water to refried beans so they can be spread. Use an 8″ × 8″ or 8″ ×10″ glass baking dish or deep glass pie pan. Start with a layer of refried beans and follow with layers of meat, cactus, sour cream, avocado, and cheese. Sprinkle black olives and chopped tomato on top. Serve with large chips.

The Great Texas Mosquito Festival: See What the Buzz Is About

The Great Texas Mosquito Festival was supposedly begun by a mosquito by the name of Willie Man-Chew in 1981 in Clute. It is said that he looked around Brazoria County, saw the human buffet there, and decided that this would be a great place to celebrate himself and his fellow bloodsuckers.

He created an annual festival in honor of himself and fellow insects, with human goodwill ambassadors he called the SWAT team. The Great Texas Mosquito Festival is held the last Thursday, Friday, and Saturday of July, and tens of thousands of people now attend. It includes games, carnival rides, crafts, a mosquito-calling contest, a beauty competition, a hay dive, and the Mr. and Mrs. Mosquito Legs Contest. The festival is covered up too, with food and cookoff competitions.

The cookoffs—the BBQ Fajita Cookoff in particular—have aroused national attention. The Food Network showed the event as part of its All-American Festivals special, which aired in 2005. The American Mosquito Control Association did a satellite feed from the festival grounds in July that same year, and the festival has been covered by USA Today, Southern Living, People, Newsweek, and more. The festival has been the topic of the Late Show with

David Letterman, CBS This Morning, and the Tonight Show.

Willie Man-Chew himself is the world's largest mosquito, standing 26 feet tall with a cowboy hat, boots, and a big stinger. He loves to pose for photos.

This July, why not take the family, leave the repellent at home, and go see what all the buzz is about?

Willie Man-Chew makes his appearance every year at the Mosquito Festival. Courtesy The Great Texas Mosquito Festival.

Red, Austin's Famous Chicken Poop Bingo Celebrity

Austin is famous for many things—its university systems, its music, and its culture—but every Sunday at Ginny's Little Longhorn Saloon, it takes on a whole new character.

The owner of the saloon, Ginny Kalmbach, has a chicken named Red. Kalmbach lets people bet on just where on a large piece of plywood, marked with numbered squares, her chicken Red will poop. She sells the 52 chances for $2.00 each, and when everyone's placed their bets, Kalmbach sets Red on the plywood, which is up high enough for everyone to see, because she has the board placed on a pool table. It is there that Red makes someone's day.

The winner gets the kitty of $112, and the house, as they say, is always packed. Ginny's Little Longhorn Saloon is on Burnet Road, just in case you're feeling cooped up and want to get out on a Sunday afternoon.

Maybe after Red dies, Ginny will use a hen instead and everyone will place a bet on where the hen lays her egg. It could be the Sunday eggstravaganza.

But bet only if you have some eggstra money.

Texas Claims to Fame—First, Biggest, and Most

Here are just a few claims to fame held by Texas or achieved within its borders, just to give you even more to brag about when you're within earshot of anyone who's not from the Lone Star State:

The wildflower capital of Texas is the city of Temple, owing to its great number and variety of wildflower species.

The bluebird capital of Texas is the city of Wills Point. Every April, the Wills Point Bluebird Festival honors these beautiful feathered friends.

The world's largest cactus ranch is the Kactus Korral in Gonzales. It has 75 greenhouses full of cacti of all kinds and offers tours.

The hot air balloon capital of Texas is Plano, which hosts balloon races every September.

The biggest little town in the world is Ozona. It's the only town in Crockett County, which covers 3,215 square miles!

The oldest town in Texas is Nacogdoches, which was a settlement as long ago as 1716. Although six flags have flown over the rest of Texas, according to the Texas Department of Transportation, nine (including three ill-fated republics) have flown over Nacogdoches. The city also is home to the oldest public thoroughfare in the entire country: La Calle del Norte, or "the Street of the North."

The world's greatest quantity of helium is in Amarillo. There you'll find the Helium Monument, a six-story-tall column of stainless steel commemorating this fact, and a helium technology exhibit at the Don Harrington Discovery Center on Streit Drive.

The world's largest livestock exposition is the Houston Livestock Show and Rodeo, held every March.

The world's largest jackrabbit is known as Jack Ben Rabbit. This fiberglass statue measures eight feet tall and is on display on North Sam Houston Avenue in Odessa.

The world's largest peanut is in Pearsall, which grows not only a huge amount of peanuts but potatoes too. The artificial peanut, roughly the size of a Mazda Miata (my car), stands on a white concrete base on Oak Street. The white base reads: "Pearsall, Texas/World's Largest Peanut/55,000,000 lbs. marketed annually." Yes, that is 55 million pounds. If I grew and marketed that much, guess I would be nutty not to brag about it.

The world largest pecan is in the town of Seguin, and is actually a 1,000-pound concrete statue of a pecan. Also in this city you will find what is probably the largest collection of nutcrackers (6,000 and counting, according to owner Kenneth Pape). You can see them at Pape Pecan House, a shop that sells everything related to pecans.

The spinach capital of the world is Crystal City, which has a statue of the famous spinach-eating sailor man, Popeye, in front of city hall. The town hosts at least two festivals celebrating its designation.

The world's longest watermelon-seed-spitting distance is currently held by Lee Wheelis of Luling. A speed-spitting contest is part of the town's Watermelon Thump (they say they wanted to come up with a name that sounded "just like fun"), held the last full weekend of every June. The distance Wheelis covered with the aid of his talented tongue was 68 feet 9⅛ inches, breaking a Guinness World Record.

The world's largest watermelon is also in Luling. It's actually a water tower painted and shaped to look like a watermelon.

The world's largest strawberry weighs in at 1,600 pounds and is more than seven feet tall. The statue is on exhibit in front of the Poteet Volunteer Fire Department, in Poteet, the strawberry capital of Texas.

The world's largest roadrunner is in Fort Stockton on Main Street. Known as Paisano Pete, the statue measures 20 feet long by 11 feet tall. Your kids will get a kick out of having their photo taken alongside Pete. You can't miss him—he's perched atop a large stone wall that reads "Welcome to Fort Stockton."

The biggest Ferris wheel—in the United States, anyway—is at the site of the State Fair of Texas in Dallas. The Texas Star measures 212 feet in height, which is taller than a 20-story building. The Italian-built Ferris wheel was constructed for the 1986 World's Fair and has been in operation there ever since. The state fair is held every fall.

The world's first air-conditioned domed stadium is in Houston. The Astrodome could easily hold an 18-story building. You will remember that besides being the site of the Houston Livestock Show and Rodeo, the Astrodome made history when it became a temporary home to Hurricane Katrina refugees.

The world's largest calf-fry cook-off is held every year in Amarillo in May. Billed locally as Homer's Backyard Ball, the event was begun by agricultural engineer Travis Homer in 1997 and became part of the Make-A-Wish Foundation of the Texas Plains (a philanthropic effort) in 2000. In 2007 the cook-off celebrated its tenth anniversary. It typically raises upwards of $30,000 annually, with an ever-increasing number of sponsors. Although it's said that the delicacy tastes a lot like chicken, maybe you should know before you go what it is that is fried at a calf fry: calf testicles. No wonder it's the world's largest—it's probably the world's only.

The world's largest indoor air-conditioned pedestrian tunnel is the Houston Tunnel System, a seven-mile system of interconnecting underground tunnels and skywalks that leads to shops, restaurants, and hotels.

The water-recreation capital of Texas is Canyon Lake and the surrounding area (just north and slightly east of San Antonio). You can participate in more than a half-dozen water-based activities in one day here, thanks to the U.S. Army Corps of Engineers, which built the lake in the mid-1960s.

The oldest "new" gorge in the world is a title that—as of press time, anyway—would have to go to Canyon Lake Gorge. In what scientists call a flood event in 2002, waters created a gorge measuring 1.5 miles long and nearly 80 feet deep—like the Grand Canyon but on a smaller scale. The waters left exposed what had been some of earth's secrets—dinosaur footprints and other fossils dating back as far as 100 million years or more. Canyon Lake Gorge opened to limited tourism in October 2007.

The world's largest cowboy boots stand near the North Star Mall in San Antonio. The pair of lighted boots, approximately 30 feet from heel to toe, is the work of Austin artist Bob Wade.

The world's tallest statue of an American hero is the one of Sam Houston in Huntsville, standing at 67 feet.

The goose hunting capital of the world is Eagle Lake. Stephen F. Austin and his group of settlers killed an eagle there, but the goose hunting is said to be phenomenal, which makes sense because it's on the U.S. Central Flyway.

Bubbling Along

Just outside Houston lies the tiny town of Burton (population around 400, according to the Texas Department of Transportation). The people there have come up with an unusual way to raise money for the Burton Cotton Gin & Museum.

Every spring, as part of the Burton Cotton Gin Festival, the town hosts a Bubble Gum Blowing Contest, and people of all ages can enter. The proceeds for the entries go toward maintaining the museum. Even if you can't make the contest, you can tour the cotton gin museum if you give 'em a day's notice.

And if you do enter the contest, don't get too nervous. You don't want to blow it.

So Can You Eat It? Here's an (Almost) Old Family Recipe!

This one comes from, and with the permission of, Texas Highways magazine:

Stuffed Jalapeños

Yield: 18 to 24 appetizers

By the Hamilton Pool Jalapeño Squeezers

Texas Highways photo editor Mike Murphy is a member of the Hamilton Pool Jalapeño Squeezers, a group of friends who enjoys competing in barbecue cook-offs. The group agreed to share one of its award-winning recipes; however, Mike cautions: "You might want to wear some disposable food-service gloves when preparing these appetizers, and don't rub your eyes or anything else!" He adds, "These are fun to serve at parties—they tend to separate the real Texans from the wannabes!"

18 to 24 large, fresh jalapeños

1 smoked chicken breast (precooked), finely chopped

1 onion, finely chopped

1 bunch cilantro, finely chopped

1 package (8 ounces) cream cheese, softened

2 teaspoons Tony Chachere's Original Seasoning

½ teaspoon salt

½ teaspoon pepper

Juice of 1 lime

1/3 cup chopped pecans (optional)

1 pound bacon (either thin- or thick-sliced)

Sturdy round toothpicks

Directions: Slice each jalapeño lengthwise, from the tip of the pepper to below the stem, almost in half, so that you can open it like a clam. Remove seeds and veins, using a small melon scooper or spoon. Wash jalapeños, making sure to wash away any remaining seeds.

Combine chopped chicken breast, onion, and cilantro in a medium-size bowl to make the stuffing for the peppers. Add cream cheese, seasonings, and lime juice (and pecans, if desired), and mix well; set aside.

Remove 9 to 12 pieces of bacon from package, cut pieces in half (each length of bacon will wrap 2 peppers), and set aside. (Reserve remaining bacon for another use.)

Using a spoon, fill each jalapeño with stuffing, and then squeeze the pepper closed. Scrape off excess stuffing, then wrap a length of bacon around pepper, and secure it by inserting a toothpick all the way through. (Any remaining stuffing makes an excellent dip.) Refrigerate peppers (overnight, if necessary) until ready to cook.

Prepare charcoal fire. (Peppers may also be deep-fried, if you prefer.) When ready, grill peppers, turning often, about 10 minutes, or until bacon looks done, then serve.

It's a Mirage—It's a Prada Store! Or Is It?

About 30 miles from the small artists' community of Marfa (population just over 2,000), there's not much to see on this lonely stretch of highway (U.S. Highway 90). German artists Michael Elmgreen and Ingar Dragset decided to add a surprising touch to the desolate landscape.

What they created, dubbed Prada Marfa, is an adobe building stocked with Prada purses and shoes. You can only look at it—it's sealed—and appreciate this haute couture mirage for its artistic merit.

Doin' Time in . . . an Art Museum?

In the city of Albany (population roughly 2,000), you will find an ancient limestone jailhouse, built in 1877. It closed in 1929—for corrective purposes, anyway—and is now renovated, serving the town as an art museum.

The old building was re-created to house art by the Old Foundation and since its reopening in 1980 has shown works created by such notable artists as Paul Klee and Pablo Picasso.

Might be a nice way to spend some . . . time on your hands.

For People Who Remember Spam as Something Other Than What's in Their E-mail In-Box

The city of Austin holds an annual celebration in honor of Spam, the canned pork product. Austin residents David Arnsberger and Dick Terry came up with the idea for Spamarana, which has such events as the Spamalympics, a Spam-calling competition (something like hog calling), and of course, a Spam cook-off.

Arnsberger and Terry started the event as an alternative to spring barbecue festivals. It was initially held in a place called Soap Creek Saloon but has grown so much that it now takes places in Austin's Waterloo Park.

Begun in 1976, Spamarana is held on various weekends each spring. Not only do the attendees have a squealing good time but also part of each year's proceeds now go toward helping disabled Central Texans in need.

New Year's Tradition or Marketing Ploy?

Back in 1947, there was a man named Elmore Torn Sr. who was hired to work for the Henderson County Chamber of Commerce for the purpose of boosting the town's economy. Torn looked around the county for ideas—there were farm crops, oil, a pottery business, and a cannery. One of the products canned there was black-eyed peas.

Back then, the canning process hadn't yet been perfected, so promoting anything canned was a challenge in itself. Torn came up with an idea: promote the concept of eating black-eyed peas on New Year's Day to ensure good luck.

Torn didn't stop there: He tied in the still-burning South-versus-North rivalry, claiming that after the Civil War, Northerners tried to suppress what Torn claimed was a fine Southern tradition, the eating of black-eyed peas on New Year's Day. In some fliers he printed through the chamber, Torn appealed to all Southerners: Why not revive this fine old nearly lost tradition—and get canned black-eyed peas from, of all places, Henderson County?

Just after Thanksgiving, Torn mailed the fliers, along with small cans of black-eyed peas, to food editors of major Southern newspapers, and continued to do so until the buzz caught on, and suddenly everyone believed that it was indeed an old Southern tradition to have black-eyed peas on New Year's Day. The rest, as they say, is history.

Next New Year's Day when you eat your black-eyed peas, thank Elmore Torn Sr. of Henderson County for this new "old" tradition.

Incidentally, there is a bit more to this story: The son of Elmore Torn Sr. became the famous actor Elmore Torn Jr. You might know him better as Rip Torn.

Strange But True!

The Texas Chainsaw Massacre Fan Club

In the late 1990s, a man named Tim Harden became so fascinated with the Texas Chainsaw Massacre (TCM) movies that he ultimately started a cult following of them. He first saw a version of TCM with friends when he was 16 and in high school, and, he says now, he still remembers how deeply it affected him.

The first movie was simply called Texas Chainsaw Massacre. Years later Harden and his wife, Cheri, moved from San Antonio to Austin, where they learned that TCM was filmed in Austin. This was around 1997–1998, and Harden began sending out e-mails searching for the site of the house in the film. "I discovered a map...," he recalls now, "and one morning my wife and I went to find it, even jumped a couple of barbed wire fences." To their dismay, the house had been moved.

Harden posted the former location of site on his Web site and registered it with AltaVista, a search engine. "From there, the e-mails just poured in, about the cast, about other locations such as the cemetery, the gas station, etc.," he says. "The Web site grew and grew to what it is now."

The greatest benefit of the work is that Harden has become good friends with the cast members, and quite a few relationships have bloomed as a result. He still has his job in telecommunications but enjoys giving tours of the film sites. He says that the tours "are fun because I get to talk shop with Chainsaw fans about how the movies were made, and I see myself as something more than just a fan." He says that he really enjoys talking with people about what the cast members are like, and it gives the fans a sense of reality about the movie. "When they see the location, they go back to the film, and it opens a new dimension to the viewing," he added.

Both Harden and his wife get "a big kick out of" giving tours and interacting with the fans. His latest big project was the largest-ever reunion of TCM cast members in Mesquite, in March 2007. New Line Cinema has also been talking about a miniseries, and Harden wants to publish a TCM cookbook, with cast members' favorite recipes and photographs.

Incidentally, a Texas chain-saw massacre never really happened—it was inspired by a grisly case in Wisconsin, however—and there was never a chain saw involved in the true story. Guess it just makes it more interesting if you have a chain saw, and Texas, involved.

All Eyes Are On You at This Barbecue Place!

In Columbus, there's a barbecue restaurant that may leave you feeling as if you're being watched. There's a reason for this.

Jerry Mikeska's Bar-B-Que Catering Service has nearly 200 animals stuffed and mounted on the restaurant walls. The animals include moose, goats, one chicken, deer, elk, fish, mountain lions, and even a cape buffalo. At the front door you're greeted with a pair of stuffed bears, standing upright on their back legs and holding baskets.

Though Mikeska is a hunter, most of his taxidermic items were purchased from others who wanted to get rid of their hunting trophies—so when your spouse starts making noises about shedding your own wall trophies, at least you've got a place to sell 'em.

Crawford, Where You Can Pose with the (Cardboard) President

A shop called the Coffee Station in Crawford, Texas, has as one of its claims to fame an offer to let you pose for a photo of President George W. Bush himself—almost.

The town of Crawford is near the Bush ranch, and locals refer to it as the Western White House. To play on this, the Coffee Station has cardboard likenesses of George W. and his father, former president George H.W. Bush, along with his wife, former First Lady Barbara Bush.

President Bush has visited the Coffee Station several times, the owners say, and has enjoyed their food.

The Coffee Station sells other president-related paraphernalia such as presidential coffee mugs, T-shirts, and caps—and President Bush has even been spotted in the vicinity jogging, wearing their T-shirt.

When you go for coffee here, you're getting a lot more than a latte.

Come Celebrate Thanksgiving in El Paso—in April!

You may have noticed that Texans have a way of celebrating their uniqueness. That goes for celebrating holidays too. The time of year that the citizens of El Paso celebrate Thanksgiving is unique as well—but they have a reason for it.

Long ago, an expedition of Spanish explorers, headed by Juan de Oñate y Salazar, came to the area now known as El Paso. The trip was arduous, and when they successfully crossed the Rio Grande, they paused and had a big feast in thanksgiving for a safe journey.

That was in April 20, 1598, and now the people of El Paso continue to celebrate their Thanksgiving not only in November but also in April.

The Best of the Wurst

The Best of the Wurst is celebrated in New Braunfels. This sausage festival takes place every November.

There Are Only So Many Hours in a Day

The Red River County Courthouse in Clarksville has in its bell tower a clock affectionately named Old Red. Installed when the courthouse was completed in 1885, the clock ran without a proverbial hitch until 1961, when it was updated to run on electricity.

Apparently Old Red didn't like the wattage and one night, gonged repeatedly—120 times to be exact—and the clock had to be unplugged before the gonging would stop. Locals call this the "night it got later than ever before" in their town.

When Laredo Was Its Own Country . . . and Still (Kind of) Is

Laredo—now a bustling city of more than 177,000 people—was once its own country. It was here that the Republic of the Rio Grande was established for a short period of time. Begun in 1839, the republic was no more in 1841.

Laredo today often still feels as though it is a country unto itself: Because it is the gateway to Mexico, you get the sense of living in another country as you take in the ambience. Also, unlike any other city in the Lone Star State, Laredo celebrates Washington's birthday—and I mean really celebrates. They began celebrating the birthday of the father of our country more than a century ago, with important social events, debutantes in sparkling gowns, and extravagant parties. It's such a distinctive city that it was highlighted in a 2006 National Geographic issue.

Not Your Usual Farm

The town of McCamey (population around 2,000) in Big Bend Country was once a boomtown. When the man after which the town is named hit a gusher this desert (and deserted) area was awash overnight in oil, people, and thousands of tents.

The oil boom has long since quieted, but a new boom has come to town, in the form of a new business called West Texas Wind Farms. There are no crops here, but perched on top of the mountains in this area near U.S. Highways 67 and 385 and Farm Road 305 are hundreds of giant windmills, some with blades as long as 90 feet. Because the windmills generate the largest amount of wind energy in the United States, West Texas Wind Farms has made another name for McCamey: the wind energy capital of Texas.

And Speaking of Wind . . .

Windmills helped settle Texas because they brought up water from deep in the Earth, making survival possible for early settlers. This is not lost on the people of Texas, and the windmill is remembered in two unusual museums in the state.

The Dutch Windmill Museum in Nederland is both to commemorate the windmills that made life possible for early Texans and to preserve Dutch heritage (many Dutch as well as French settled in this area). This museum also houses mementos of the famous country singer, Tex Ritter, and the Olympic gold medal won in Finland's 1952 competition by W.F. "Buddy" Davis, both of whom lived in Nederland.

Lubbock is the place where you'll find the American Wind Power Center, which is a 28-acre museum featuring more than 75 windmills of all descriptions and sizes, with exhibits both inside and outside the building.

Remembering Those Forgotten

The Holocaust may seem like a piece long-ago history to many, but not for the people of Houston. Many Europeans arrived on American shores in the aftermath of World War II and its havoc, and some of those made new lives for themselves in Texas. In Houston, on Caroline Street, you will find an interactive memorial dedicated to those who died in the Holocaust and those who survived it—the Holocaust Museum Houston. The museum also remembers the most innocent of the victims in a butterfly exhibit, with each butterfly dedicated to the memory of a child who died in the Holocaust.

Dallas also is home to the Dallas Holocaust Museum/Center for Education & Tolerance, located on North Record Street. The center offers guided tours of exhibits relating to this tragic, historic time.

If You're from Texas, You're from . . . Everywhere

Texans embrace pretty much everybody, no matter where they're from, because the majority of Texans have their roots in other lands. Take the Plains city of Panna Maria: It's the oldest permanent Polish settlement in the United States, and the school there—St. Joseph School—which is now a museum, is the oldest private Polish school in the country.

In the Panhandle Plains area, the town of Shamrock celebrates its Irish citizenry with a piece of Ireland: In Elmore Park, you can actually kiss a part of a stone that came from Blarney Castle in County Cork. This ensures "everlasting good luck" for the kisser.

The town of Center has a nineteenth-century courthouse modeled after an Irish castle, complete with turrets and towers. The city of Caldwell has so many Czech settlers that it has been named the "kolache capital of Texas" by the state legislature. (A kolache is a kind of sandwich or sometimes a sweet pastry.) Caldwell also has the Burleson County Czech Heritage Museum in town, located in the chamber of commerce building. The town of Flatonia lends a Czech flavor to its chili festival by calling it Czhilispiel. To take this a step further, the town of West (which, ironically, is located in central Texas) has been recognized by the state legislature as the "Czech heritage capital of Texas."

The city of Clifton has been named the "Norwegian capital of Texas" by the 1977 state legislature, and its Bosque Museum contains the largest collection of Norwegian artifacts in this part of the country. Clifton goes even further to celebrate its Norse heritage, with such events as Norwegian Constitution Day every May and a smorgasbord festival every November. A well-known Norwegian in Hamilton, Elise Waerenskjold, was an outspoken author, writing against slavery and for temperance.

The city of Ennis celebrates its German heritage with its annual National Polka Festival, held every Memorial Day weekend, and the town of Independence is known as the first permanent German settlement in Texas.

Q & A

Q. What town in the Panhandle used to be known as "uplift city" and why?

A. The city of McLean, because it used to be home to a brassiere factory.

Q. What city had an all-volunteer traveling circus that operated from 1930 until the 1960s?

A. Gainesville. The Santa Fe Depot Museum there has exhibits relating to the circus.

Q. What city is home to Texas's oldest continually operating theater?

A. Corpus Christi. The theater is the Harbor Playhouse.

Q. What area of Texas offers one of the most spectacular theater experiences in the nation, the musical Texas—outdoors?

A. Palo Duro Canyon offers this musical play every June through August in its Pioneer Amphitheater.

Q. How did the city of Iraan (in Big Bend Country) get its name?

A. The combination of the names of Ira and Ann Yates, the owners of the land on which the town sits, created the name.

Q. What famous comic strip Neanderthal-type caveman was created by artist V.T. Hamlin?

A. Alley Oop, from the comic strip of the same name. There is a giant figure of the character in Fantasyland Park in Iraan, which is where the artist lived at one time.

Q. What claim to fame is held by the Chris Davidson Memorial Park in Midland?

A. It is one of only three parks in the United States that is totally accessible by wheelchair.

Q. What hatchery, located in Lake Jackson, has the capacity to produce more than 20 million fingerlings of (mostly) red drum and spotted sea trout annually?

A. Sea Center Texas.

Q. Where in Texas will you find a collection of cars made to look like whimsical pieces of art—such as a rabbit?

A. The Art Car Museum in Houston, which has as part of its collection a Volkswagen Beetle made to look like a giant polyester rabbit, and a motorcycle made to look like a woman's red stiletto heel.

Q. For what is the Big Texan Steak Ranch in Amarillo nationally famous?

A. For its 72-ounce steak. It's free if you can eat it all in less than an hour.

Q. What city has preserved as part of its cultural heritage a section called Old Irishtown?

A. Corpus Christi. The area has many restored early-twentieth-century homes and has the Institute of Cultures, celebrating the city's heritage.

Q. Where is the site of Texas's first Mardi Gras celebration?

A. Menard Home, which is also Galveston's oldest home, built in 1838

Q. Where was the site of and what was the name of Texas's first free public library?

A. Galveston; Rosenberg Library

Q. What city was designated as "the mural capital of Texas" by the Texas Legislature in January 2001?

A. Breckenridge, with at least eight (and counting) incredibly realistic murals depicting the town's and the state's history, at major intersections.

Q. For what is New Braunfels native Ferdinand Jakob Lindheimer (1801–1879) famous?

A. He was the first to classify the majority of Texas flora.

His home is now open for tours.

Q. What town holds one of the oldest annual events in Texas, the Yamboree, celebrating the sweet potato?

A. Gilmer.

Q. Where is the Women's Museum, honoring such notables as Margaret Mead, Barbara Jordan, and Eleanor Roosevelt?

A. In Fair Park, on Parry Avenue, in Dallas.

Q. What city could be called "the Smithsonian of Texas," and why?

A. Fort Worth, because it has more museums than any other city in the southwestern United States!

Q. What city is home to the Texas State Championship Domino Tournament?

A. Hallettsville.

UNUSUAL GRAVE AND BURIAL-SITE STORIES

Buried (Pre)History . . .

Approximately 28,000 years ago near present-day Waco, where the Brazos and Bosque rivers meet, a herd of mammoths came to drink. Scientists think that while the mammoths were imbibing, a thunderstorm sprang up, the riverbank gave way, and the 24 mammoths were buried in the earth.

There are many prehistoric animals being unearthed in Texas. A pterodactyl like this one probably flew over Texas long before any flag did. Courtesy, Wikipedia.

The place where they met their fate has now been excavated and is—so far—the largest mammoth archeological site in the world. Texans haven't kept this prehistoric treasure for themselves: You can go see the mammoth exhibit, called the Waco Mammoth Experience, which is part of the Mayborn Museum Complex.

. . . and Buried Horsepower

In 1974, one of the more colorful of Amarillo's residents, eccentric millionaire Stanley Marsh 3, decided to create a quirky "graveyard" of his own. Near Interstate 40, Marsh buried 10 classic, ancient Cadillacs, nose down, tail fins in the air. (The Texas Department of Transportation says that these Caddies were made to rest in the same angle as the Cheops pyramids in Egypt—a connection I never could discern). Known as Cadillac Ranch, the place attracts visitors from all over the world. Visitors have been known to decorate the Caddies for holidays such as Christmas.

Author Paul H. Carlson, who wrote an authoritative text on all things Amarillo (Amarillo: The Story of a Western Town, Texas Tech University Press), wrote of Cadillac Ranch: ". . . in a time-honored tradition, [visitors] leave their mark with felt-tip pens or spray paint [on the cars]."

Is there meaning here—a statement made? Perhaps. One journalist described Cadillac Ranch as the "Panhandle's answer to the Statue of Liberty." Marsh explains this and his other artistic efforts as a "legalized form of insanity," according to Frommer's Travel Guide online magazine.

Cadillac Ranch is open to the public.

Strange But True!

Funerary Finds

If you want to see the largest collection of memorabilia related to all things funerary, check out the National Museum of Funeral History in Houston. Included in its collection is a funeral sleigh, horse-drawn hearses, and a Packard funeral (mourning) bus that once could transport 20 funeral attendants, pallbearers, and the casket all at the same time.

A Mysterious Burial Site in Aurora

Long before the U.S. government, or anyone else, had other technological excuses for UFOs—such as experimental aircraft—there was a strange crash of an unidentified flying object in the tiny town of Aurora.

The year was 1897—before the Wright brothers' historic flight in North Carolina—but whatever the aircraft was, it crashed into a windmill after first being seen flying over the town square. Although the single inhabitant—presumably the pilot—was the only victim of the crash, E.E. Haydon, writer of the story on the crash for the April 19 edition of the Dallas Morning News that year said, on the basis of the pilot's features, that the body was "not of this world." Whether the pilot was of this world or not, the proper people of Aurora gave the body a burial, complete with headstone, in Aurora Cemetery.

Years passed. The incident, ignored by the media worldwide, suddenly was the focus of a resurgence in interest, probably ignited when the headstone was stolen. By this time, enough years had passed that no one remembered just exactly where in the cemetery the alien pilot was buried. Others became intrigued by the possibility that a UFO had crashed on American soil in the nineteenth century, and in the mid-1970s, the International UFO Bureau requested of the Aurora Cemetery Association permission to seek out and exhume the pilot's body for further investigation. The association blocked such attempts, and although the International UFO Bureau tried again for the same thing in 2005, they were rebuffed.

The strange crash and burial—not to mention identification—of this body continues to be a source of mystery and debate, and although it has been aired on such television shows as Sightings and in a special presentation on the History Channel, no answers have been forthcoming—only questions. In 1976 Texas erected a historical marker at the cemetery, mentioning the "alien burial," so apparently the state is aware of the curious nature of the crash and burial.

The town of Aurora is approximately 10 miles outside Fort Worth—just in case you want to visit the cemetery and pay your respects.

Free at Last—Underground

"Inmates who die in the Texas prison system," wrote Jim Willett on the Texas Prison Museum Web site (see the "Virtual Texas" section near the back of this book), "are buried there [in Captain Joe Byrd Cemetery] for one reason—no one claims the body."

In Huntsville, on virtually every Monday through Thursday, inmates' bodies unclaimed by family members are put to rest in Joe Byrd Cemetery. In its early days, no records were kept of what had once been referred to as Peckerwood Hill, named thus for the poorest inmates, called peckerwoods by fellow inmates. Burial of these poorest-of-the-poor inmates on this 22-acre plot had gone on since its inception in 1855, but little or no maintenance of the cemetery was done until more than 100 years later.

In 1962 Assistant Warden Captain Joe Byrd took it upon himself to begin cleaning up and properly maintaining the cemetery. Although his plan included identifying the graves, he and his workers were successful in identifying only about 900 such graves; more than 300 remain unidentified.

Now the cemetery, renamed the Captain Joe Byrd Cemetery, is beautifully maintained and open for public tours. It sits on a placid hill on Bowers Boulevard.

The Saddest Day: The New London School Explosion

Mention the words school explosion to 99 percent of Texans and they will know what you mean. The explosion, a combination of human error and bad timing, resulted in more than 300 teachers and schoolchildren being killed in the blink of an eye on a terrible day in March 1937.

This was not the act of a terrorist but a lack of judgment. The New London School, one of the best schools in the state because of the wealth of oil in the area, was built complete with the first football stadium to have electric lights. It also was built over a large dead-air space, a decision that would prove deadly. When, in an effort to save money, the school board opted to cancel its natural gas contract and tap into a residue gas line (which was usually simply burned off), the combination of these two decisions resulted in tragedy.

Grades 1 through 4 had been let out early the day of March 18, 1937, and parents were involved in a Parent Teacher Association meeting in the nearby gymnasium. At this time in history, natural gas had nothing added to it to help people detect a leak. Schoolchildren had been complaining of headaches, and this was the only clue, in retrospect, that showed that the leak had been building up.

When a worker turned on an electric sander at 3:05 pm, the spark ignited the gas-filled air. Surviving witnesses say that the school's walls bulged outward, and then the roof lifted off the building before slamming back down. Of the 600 students and roughly 40 faculty members in the building, only approximately 130 escaped without injury. The rest were wounded or killed.

Because the loud explosion was heard for miles, no one needed an alarm to know that a disaster was at hand. Oil-field workers, called roughnecks, came to help clear debris, working with frantic parents to find their children. Media also arrived but were asked to help instead of report what they saw. One of these was a cub reporter named Walter Cronkite, who said in later years that it was the worst tragedy he ever covered.

Surrounding communities were made into morgues, taking in the dead—or oftentimes, pieces of bodies. There was not a family in the town unaffected by the disaster.

Today, another school stands near the location of the old school. It has a new name—West Rusk High School—and a monument stands on Texas State Highway 42 in memory of those who lost their lives that terrible day.

I like to think, as many do, that these children and teachers did not die in vain. In the wake of this disaster, the state of Texas called for a compound called thiol to be added to natural gas. This idea took hold worldwide and has undoubtedly saved many lives, with its disagreeable odor indicating a gas leak.

Most of the victims of this tragedy now rest in Pleasant Hill Cemetery. The survivors and their families are still reluctant to talk about it, but the son of one of them has formed a Web site for survivors, family members, and interested parties (see the "Virtual Texas" section near the back of this book).

Next to the Galveston hurricane of 1900 and the Texas City explosion of 1947 (see story, below), the New London School explosion remains the third-deadliest tragedy in the Lone Star State.

The Gentleman Gunfighter

In Pecos, Texas, you can visit the West of the Pecos Museum and see all the fascinating artifacts there, including the place where two outlaws were killed by bartender Barney Riggs. You can tour a full 50 rooms of all kinds of exhibits relating to the early days of Pecos and Texas history.

One of the things you might not want to miss, though, is a tombstone. It's in the park adjacent to the museum. Here is the burial place of the "Gentleman Gunfighter," Clay Allison.

In his day, he had a quick temper, because, some said, of an old head injury. He was equally as quick with a pistol as he was with a knife, and woe to anyone who angered or challenged Allison. One man who did so wound up literally losing his head; another, a dentist who drilled the wrong tooth, lost part of his lip. He fought in the Civil War. Reading about his misdeeds, anyone might wonder why the South didn't win with a hot-tempered soldier like him on its side.

The last fight of his life took place right before July 1, 1887, the day Allison was killed. He and another man had gotten into a dispute, and Allison decided to settle it in an unusual way. Legend has it that together they dug a grave, agreeing to meet at a specific time to fight it out, inside the empty grave, to the death, naked and armed with only Bowie knives. The loser would get the grave; the winner would climb out.

Just before the decisive fight was to take place, Allison was on his wagon with a load of grain when he fell off the wagon and one of the wheels rolled over his neck, breaking it and killing him instantly. He was buried on July 4, 1887, on the grounds that are now part of the museum and park, near the tourist center and the Pecos Area Chamber of Commerce.

Locals say that his former tombstone boasted these words: "I never killed a man who didn't need it." According to "outlaw specialist" Charley Eckhardt at Texas Escapes, that tombstone was stolen; the replacement simply bears the name Robert C. Allison and his date of death, and mentions his service to the Confederate States of America. When you visit Pecos, go by the museum and the park and pay your respects to the man Texas knows as the "Gentleman Gunfighter."

Stephen F. Austin: Buried Twice

The founder of Texas's first capital when it was a republic was not always buried in Austin. When he passed away in West Columbia (in what is known now as the Brazosport area), he was taken down the Brazos River to Peach Point Plantation. In what is known today as Jones Creek, Austin's body was buried in Gulf Prairie Cemetery.

The powers that be at the time, apparently, wanted to have Austin's remains placed in the town named after him, so in 1910, his remains were moved to Austin by wagon, where he is buried in the state cemetery.

DID YOU KNOW?

Famous Texans: Where Are They Buried?

Two authors—Robert Howard, writer of the Conan the Barbarian stories, and Katherine Anne Porter, best known for her Ship of Fools—are interred in Brownwood, in the Panhandle Plains.

Planning Ahead

President George W. Bush's father, former president George H.W. Bush, has chosen his burial site: the grounds of the George Bush Presidential Library and Museum, which is in College Station, Brazos County. The library and museum is an impressive 69,000 square feet and is open to the public.

The Buried Past Lives On: Jefferson Davis Hospital

There is an area of Houston that is said to be the burial grounds of an old English settlement that existed around the late 1500s or early 1600s that contains the bodies of those who died of the bubonic plague. When it was made into a cemetery for the city of Houston in 1840, it was named simply City Cemetery. During the Civil War, both Union and Confederate soldiers were also laid to rest there. According to articles in the Houston Chronicle dating as far back as 1993, the last person buried in City Cemetery was laid to rest in 1904, but as many as 6,000 people have been buried there.

Jefferson Davis Hospital: haunted or not? Courtesy Michael Edwards/Houston Haunts.

In 1924, construction began on the Jefferson Davis Hospital—right over the burial grounds. Over the years, the hospital went through several incarnations, from a charity hospital to a juvenile detention facility to a rehabilitation clinic, and even a psychiatric hospital. Abandoned for years and in a terrible state of disrepair, the hospital named after the president of the Confederate States of America has been completely renovated. The building now contains high-priced, trendy lofts.

Although it is said that most of the bodies were moved during construction of the hospital, some people in the Houston area say that the building is still haunted—by the spirits of former doctors, nurses, psychiatric patients, and soldiers. According to the Houston Chronicle, there are more than 100 different spiritual beings who occupy the Jefferson Davis Hospital.

Sometimes it's not always possible to bury the past. It may live on in the Jefferson Davis Hospital.

A Final Resting Place for Seminole Scouts

Back when the United States was being settled by Europeans, many Native Americans who could sit a horse well and were handy with a rifle were recruited to be scouts for the U.S. Army. Oftentimes—tragically—when they had served their purpose, these scouts were often relieved of their uniforms and guns and sent to live on reservations with the rest of the peoples they had, ironically enough, helped move there.

Some of these scouts were from the Seminole tribe and had left their Oklahoma reservation. The U.S. Army hired approximately 150 such indigenous men as scouts to trail other marauding tribespeople who were an "annoyance" to the federal government.

Four of these scouts won Medals of Honor from the government for their service; most of these are buried in a cemetery in the town of Brackettville, east of Del Rio, and their descendants, who now live in the area, maintain the site.

Q & A

Q. What cemetery in Texas is referred to as "the Arlington of Texas," and why?

A. The Texas State Cemetery in Austin, which contains the remains of almost 2,000 people important in Texas history—settlers, politicians, and heroes. Besides marking the resting places of such icons as Stephen F. Austin and Confederate States of America General Albert Sidney Johnston, there is a fairly recent memorial, honoring those who died in the tragedy of September 11, 2001.

Q. Who wrote Sam Houston's epitaph, where is his grave located, and how does it read?

A. The epitaph was written by Andrew Jackson. At his grave site in Oakwood Cemetery in Huntsville, Texas, it reads: "The world will take care of Houston's fame."

Q. What cemetery in Nacogdoches contains the graves of four signers of the Texas Declaration of Independence?

A. Oak Grove Cemetery.

Q. In what city will you find the oldest known Anglo grave in Texas?

A. Clarksville, Texas, has in its borders a historical marker along Farm Road 410 commemorating the grave of Jane Chandler Gill.

Q. Where is Jesse James buried?

A. In Granbury Cemetery, Granbury, Texas.

T★X
CHAPTER
14

LIGHTHOUSE AND COASTAL STORIES

Strange But True!

Bolivar Lighthouse, the Target of Friendly Fire

In 1917 places all around the coastal United States were on alert to be on the lookout for possible enemy attack. The lighthouses along the coast of Texas were no exception.

Bolivar Lighthouse. Courtesy Bolivar Peninsula Chamber of Commerce.

At that time, the lighthouse keeper for Bolivar Lighthouse was a man named Harry Claiborne, who was justifiably alarmed when the lighthouse began being shelled one afternoon in November. He contacted the U.S. Coast Guard to determine who the assailant was, and they and naval commanders came in time to see shells falling somewhat short of their target. The next day Claiborne learned that the barrage was not from the enemy but was friendly fire from nearby Fort San Jacinto. Soldiers were practicing their aims with nonexplosive shells using old ammunition and never dreamed that some of the shells would even come close to the lighthouse.

Avast, Ye Maties! A Museum Just for Us, Argh!

In the 1970s, Ron Francis William Dowling operated a pirate museum on the Isle of Wight in England. Apparently, his son John always thought it would be more fitting to have the pirate museum located on the shores of the southern United States, especially after reading accounts of pirates such as Jean Lafitte who patrolled the waters and terrorized the seas around Corpus Christi Bay.

When Dowling passed away in 2003, son John Dowling moved every bit of the collection of swords, cannonballs, pirate booty, and the like, to the Gulf Coast—Padre Island, specifically—and it operates today as the Pirate and Smuggling Museum. Visitors are enthralled by displays of more than 300 pirate artifacts, smuggled objects, and mannequin displays showing pirates in various historical representations of prosecution for their misdeeds. Some artifacts date back to the 1580s.

DID YOU KNOW?

A Lightship?

The first lighthouse in operation along the shore of Texas wasn't a lighthouse at all, but a lightship. Placed at anchor on a sandbar at the port of Galveston in 1849, the lightship was the first federally funded maritime navigational aid on the Texas coast. It was followed by a lighthouse at Matagorda in 1852, then another at Bolivar Point on Galveston Bay.

The so-called Galveston Lightship lit the way for maritime navigators from the year of its inception until 1860, when it sank in the harbor. Its successor, another lightship built in Norfolk, Virginia, continued the service of saving maritime travelers from 1870, and for the next

35 years did so, except when it was under repair. Finally, the old lightship was deemed decrepit and was sent to the salvage yard.

Pristine Padre Island

Of the 110 miles that comprise Padre Island, 80 miles of it—the National Seashore—is preserved in its natural state, making this one of the largest such seashores in the country. Furthermore, the Padre Island National Seashore has the longest stretch of undeveloped barrier-island beach property in the entire world.

Spring-Break Beach

South Padre Island has been listed as one of the top 10 beaches for spring-break vacationers. The area has more than 100,000 visitors during spring break alone. Although it's separated by the Texas mainland by 2½ miles, many vacationers feel as though they're no longer in the United States at all.

Goin' Back to Houston . . .

If we heard the Dean Martin rendition of the song "Goin' Back to Houston," we'd be singing along in agreement. Named after Sam Houston, who won Texas's independence from Mexico (see "Remember the Alamo!" in Chapter 3, "Before 'the' War") and who was also the president of the Republic of Texas, the city of Houston has a lot to be proud of. From its humble beginnings as a riverboat landing in 1836, today Houston is a bustling coastal city— the fourth largest in the United States and the largest city in Texas, period.

Rockport

The lovely town of Rockport, across the water from St. Joseph Island, is popular today for its scenic beauty, its friendliness to tourists (whether they're fishing or bird-watching), and its hospitality. In the 1940s, however, it was a town of strategic importance to World War II.

Before the war turned people's minds to doing their part for the United States and the free world, the two shipyards in Rockport built small marine craft such as sailboats and skiffs, which boaters took to the nearby waters of Copano and Aransas bays. When German submarines began sabotaging Atlantic Ocean shipping lanes, however, it was time for action.

President Franklin D. Roosevelt gave an official order for a large-scale rearmament; this included contracts for suppliers of all kinds of goods and services—including shipbuilding. One of the shipbuilding companies in Rockport, Westergard-Rice Brothers and Co., applied for and received one of the contracts. Their mission: build sub chasers to defend the shipping lanes against the German submarines.

The first was completed and launched on Independence Day 1941—months before the attack on Pearl Harbor. The little shipyard produced a sub chaser every six months on average. These clunky-looking wooden-hulled ships went to sea with a handful of enlisted men and three officers—what a gunner's-mate-turned poet, O.E. Moore, described in 1942 as "wooden ships with iron men"—and helped bring victory for the United States.

Today, when you visit the Rockport–Fulton area, you can learn more about the sub chasers by visiting the Texas Maritime Museum at Rockport Harbor.

The Ellis Island of the West

Besides being the only major port facility in the country not supported by public funds, the Port of Galveston has earned the nickname "Ellis Island of the West" because of the large number of immigrants who entered

America through it. Many of your ancestors may have come to the United States this way, so if you haven't had any luck checking New York immigration records, go to Galveston's Texas Seaport Museum, where they'll let you research information on more than 130,000 immigrants. While you're there, check out the museum's centerpiece: Elissa, a barkentine tall ship, built in Scotland in 1877, which is not only a good example of nineteenth-century maritime technology, but is still sailing, so check for her schedule before you go.

The port's quarantine station once stood at what is now Seawolf Park, at nearby Pelican Island; many of our ancestors were probably detained here. The Texas Seaport Museum also will let you research its database online to find your ancestors (see "Virtual Texas" near the back of this book).

Lighting the Way: The Lighthouses of the Lone Star State

In was in the 1800s, and the hydrography of the Texas coastal waters could be treacherous. Because of weather and currents, the land underlying the waters could shift, causing damage and destruction to ships and life. Captains began to complain that something be done to make charting their courses safer.

In 1852, the Port Isabel Lighthouse was constructed just southwest of South Padre Island (near the Texas–Mexico border). For many years, this beacon of safety beamed a message of comfort to seafaring souls. The light shone through historical times, such as during the nearby Civil War Battle of Palmito Ranch in 1865 (the last land battle of the Civil War).

After the Civil War, people began to depend less and less on the Port Isabel Lighthouse and the other 15 lighthouses dotting the coastline of Texas. Railroads created a land route between Mexico to the south and Corpus Christi to the north, and newer technology, with lights on tall towers, made the old lighthouses a thing of the past. The Port Isabel Lighthouse's light shone for the last time in 1905.

Note the last remnants of old Fort Polk parapet in front of the structure.

Port Isabel Lighthouse, circa 1909. From left-right is the keeper's cottage and the oil-house. The lantern room was lined with blackout curtains to protect the townspeople from the light of the Fresnel lens. Lighthouse photos courtesy Rod and Valerie Bates collection.

The Great Depression of the 1930s sounded the death knell for other lighthouses as well, and Port Isabel's lighthouse fell further into disrepair. Finally, redemption came in the form of the Texas State Parks Board.

The board provided funding to repair and refurbish the Port Isabel Lighthouse in 1947, and it was finally dedicated as a state park in 1952. The lighthouse itself is also restored (the finishing touches on it were done in 2000), and many visitors have come to navigate the steps of the 72-foot lighthouse. When you go visit, you can see a replica of the old lighthouse keeper's cottage and tour the lighthouse. The keeper's cottage is now home to the Port Isabel Chamber of Commerce Visitor Center.

Hurricane Culture

People in other areas of the country may merely pause when television networks such as the Weather Channel show hurricanes as they arrive in the Gulf of Mexico. Not people in coastal areas—hurricane monitoring can, and has, become an obsession with some citizens living in harm's way during the season.

There is a kind of hurricane culture among the people living on the coast. People have to decide whether to evacuate or stay, whether to take their animals or leave them, and if they stay, what to do before a hurricane strikes. And there are the mundane concerns, such as provisioning with sufficient fuel, nonperishable food, and water. But the emotions experienced in getting ready for a hurricane's possible devastation can take a toll on the hardiest person, even before the hurricane has made landfall.

As soon as a major hurricane enters the Gulf of Mexico, people along coastlines often band together. If they don't have an electrical generator, they are obliged to clean out their freezers and cook everything so it can be merely chilled in coolers (this can take days). If they do have a generator, they will be expected to take on hurricane guests—relatives and friends who don't have generators.

In the last hours before a hurricane strikes, people who have opted to stay usually throw a hurricane party.

Hurricanes bring out the best in people (read what the citizens of Houston did to reunite New Orleans pet owners with their animals in Chapter 11, "Flora, Fauna, and Natural Phenomena"), but sometimes it brings out the worst—there is always the danger of looting and the reality of gas-price gouging.

It seems the lure of coastal living will always bring some hardy, adventurous souls to the land of sun and sand. As he was being interviewed on the Weather Channel, one Galveston resident said this in the wake of Hurricanes Katrina and, three weeks later, Rita: "This is the price we pay," he said, "for living in paradise."

The "Turtle Lady" of South Padre Island

The "Turtle Lady" was at the age where most would be sitting on a porch, simply rocking, but this feisty gem of South Padre Island, who, sadly, died in 2000, seemed to grow younger through working for a cause. For Ila Loetscher, that cause was to save and rehabilitate injured sea turtles.

With the mission to "support the conservation of all marine turtle species," as its Web site says, the organization that she established on Padre Boulevard in 1977—Sea Turtle, Inc.—actively enlists students to learn, the media to help get the word out, and teachers to enlighten their charges about how sea turtles live and how we can help them thrive in our ever-challenging environment.

Most people would have thought it would be enough to reminisce about being one of the United States' earliest female aviators and one of Amelia Earhart's contemporaries. From 1977 until her death, though, Loetscher spread her wings toward another goal of education and environmental awareness, and because of her, entire species of turtles may be saved from certain extinction.

Sea Turtle, Inc., is open to the public—but call ahead first.

Strange But True!

Visit Ancient China Without Leaving Texas

The city of Katy is home to something that you might not think of when you think of attractions in the Lone Star State. In this small town (population just under 12,000) you can feel as though you have traveled to the famed Forbidden City of China, for it is here that the Forbidden Gardens makes its home.

I was curious as to why and how a piece of China came to be located just west of Houston, and this is what I learned: "It's owned by a real estate tycoon from Hong Kong, who built it as a museum to educate his children on ancient Chinese history. He chose Katy because of its many rice paddies. When he saw the paddies, it reminded him of home," says museum director Marian Schmidt.

Schmidt says that although the Forbidden City itself is a big draw, probably 60 percent of the people who visit come to see the terra-cotta soldiers. She explained that the famous Emperor Qin (pronounced "Chin") had his servants create thousands of such soldiers, which were buried in three of the four pits at his planned burial site.

"They are about 30 inches tall, and in real life, his own soldiers were about six feet tall. Before China was unified, it was divided into seven tribes. Qin wanted to intimidate the other six tribes and make them into a unified China as we know it. He chose these tall soldiers to fight in battle against the other tribes, and upon seeing them many foes simply threw down their weapons and gave up," Schmidt says. In case you don't remember your Chinese history, Emperor Qin is responsible for building infrastructure throughout his country; he also unified the currency, gave the people Mandarin Chinese, and built the Great Wall.

Scenes from Katy's Forbidden Gardens. Courtesy Michael Morton Photography.

Forbidden Gardens is open for tours, planned group tours, special occasions, and even weddings. Check out its Web site; its address is listed in the "Virtual Texas" section near the back of this book.

When you go, prepare to be amazed!

Half-Moon Reef Lighthouse

The Half-Moon Reef Lighthouse was established in 1858 on Matagorda Bay but kept unlit during the Civil War. After the Civil War, the lighthouse began operating again, but it was badly damaged in a hurricane in 1942. The lighthouse was moved in 1943 to make room for a bombing range, then in 1979 it was moved to its present site next to the Port Lavaca Chamber of Commerce.

The Story of the *Belle*

In 1686 the *Belle* was the flagship of French explorer René-Robert Cavelier, Sieur de La Salle. La Salle had sailed his small armada of four ships in an attempt to find and establish a trading port near the mouth of the Mississippi River, giving France an economic advantage over Spain.

All might have gone well for La Salle and his crew had it not been for pirates—who commandeered one of the ships—and weather, which caused him to land on the Texas coast, some several hundred miles west of his destination. One of his ships sank in Matagorda Bay, and then the crew established a small fort to fend off the local band of hostile Karankawa Indians. Finally, one of his last remaining two ships left for France with those who did not want to stay, including some soldiers, settlers, and crewmen.

La Salle doggedly kept attempting to find a trading port, leaving his men at the fort while he furthered his search. While he was gone, the remaining crew raised the *Belle's* anchor, to attempt to cross Matagorda Bay to get help—they were running low on supplies, able-bodied seamen, and fresh water, and the Indians had killed some of the best members of the crew. They didn't make it across the bay. The *Belle* sank, most of the crew drowned, and about this time, even La Salle himself was murdered.

But that's not the end of the story about the Belle. She was discovered, deep in the mud of Matagorda Bay, some 310 years later, by J. Barto Arnold, an archeologist of the Texas Historical Commission. In an excavation, archeologists brought up the contents of the ship and finally the hull itself. The contents, basically a "colony kit on a ship," were amazingly well preserved by the mud into which they had sunk. Even rope was discovered coiled as it had been left in 1686.

It took several painstaking years to excavate and bring up everything, but now what has been under the mud in Matagorda Bay is yours to see in several exhibits in the state, including the Bob Bullock Texas State History Museum in Austin and the Texas Maritime Museum in Rockport.

There is a monument to La Salle himself in the town of Navasota.

Q & A

Q. How many miles of coastline along the Gulf of Mexico belong to Texas?

A. More than 624 miles

Q. What is the Texas coast's claim to fame when it comes to birds?

A. It's the number-one place in the nation for bird-watchers.

Q. What is the longest artificial surfing wave in the world?

A. Schlitterbahn Beach Waterpark, in South Padre Island.

Q. What bird migration is so popular in the Rockport–Fulton area that residents have created a celebration around its visits?

A. The hummingbird. Every September, the area hosts the Hummer/Bird Celebration, where bird-lovers can see the hummingbirds migrating through the area.

Q. What fort at Crystal Beach is named for a famous Alamo hero and was in heavy use during World Wars I and II?

A. Fort Travis, named for William B. Travis. Now it is known as Fort Travis Seashore Park, and is a popular tourist attraction.

Q. Where in Texas is the world's longest barrier reef?

A. Padre Island. South Padre Island, a popular tourist destination, is (of course) at its southernmost tip.

Q. What "green" idea did the people of Port Lavaca have about building materials for the walkway through their bird sanctuary?

A. The Lighthouse Beach and Bird Sanctuary's walkway is made totally out of recycled plastic!

GHOST TOWNS OF TEXAS

The Story of the War in Salt Flat

Some places have feuds over land; some have disputes over water. The citizens of Salt Flat, Texas, had a dispute over . . . well, salt.

Back in the mid-1800s salt was extracted from shallow, temporary lakes that appeared after a rain. The salt was apparently washed down from the nearby Guadalupe Mountains, and cattlemen used it to supplement the diet of their cattle. When more settlers moved in, the inevitable number of water wells drilled in the area caused the water table to fall to where the salt that was deposited dwindled to nearly nothing.

The conflict started when one group tried to lay claim to the salt flats. Citizens of the area began to fight against each other, and things went from heated to bloody in no time. The conflict lasted seven years and involved cattlemen, settlers on both sides of the Texas–Mexico border, Texas Rangers and even U.S. Army troops.

Finally, the dispute ended (with such a buildup of law enforcement, no other end was possible). To help keep the fragile peace, El Paso's Fort Bliss was established as a permanent military post.

The town of Salt Flat is now more or less a ghost town. When you go there, you can see ruins of adobe and stone houses, motels, and "tourist courts" that were bustling when Salt Flat was in its heyday.

A handful of people still live there, including a woman who, like her mother and grandmother did before her, runs the remaining one of the original two cafés in town. Shirley J. Gilmore Richardson is the woman to see there if you want to get a good meal, some conversation, and a story about the Salt Flat war.

Indianola, Destroyed by the Hand of God

Indianola was established in the 1840s on the Gulf Coast by Prince Carl of Solms-Braunfels. In the 1850s it became the site of an army depot, a hub from which all frontier forts were supplied. The determined people who settled Indianola saw the town through all types of sieges: Civil War shellings, plagues of yellow fever, and the usual hurricane seasons.

Most likely, they thought they had seen the worst that history and the weather could offer; then the hurricane of 1875 struck. Despite severe damage to the city and hundreds of lives lost in the storm, the people of Indianola rebuilt their town and their lives.

Sadly, another hurricane struck Indianola 11 years afterward, completely destroying the town. The surviving residents moved, and the county seat was relocated to Port Lavaca. (The DeWitt County Historical Museum in Cuero was built with timbers salvaged from 1886 storm.) Today, only a handful of fishing families occupy the area that was once a bustling port city, and the waves lap against the few stones that observant visitors can identify as buildings' remains. There is a historical marker on the site where the town once stood, and a statue dedicated to the French explorer who discovered this area (René-Robert Cavelier, Sieur de La Salle).

The Story of Nip and Tuck

Approximately 20 miles northeast of Henderson, there once was a town known as Nip 'n' Tuck. It was a bustling trade center in the 1850s, but when the railroads were built, they didn't go through the town. Nip 'n' Tuck declined, and a 1906 storm did away with what was left of the town. Now, only a cemetery is left of Nip 'n' Tuck, and it is known today as Harmony Hill Ghost Town.

VIRTUAL TEXAS

Internet surfers, take note: These sites were viable and accessible as of press time. Remember that computers are literal: You must type in these addresses just as they appear. Some addresses are case-sensitive; some are not. Happy surfing!

General Reference (or, If You Can't Find It Here, You Don't Need It)

Official Web site of the governor's office: www.governor.state.tx.us

Texas Escapes (all kinds of information, plus travel and columns): www.texasescapes.com

Lone Star Junction (for Texans and "foreigners" alike, the site says—very user-friendly): www.lsjunction.com

Quirky things around the Lone Star State: www.txroad-runners.com

Brownsville: www.brownsville.org

Houston: www.visithoustontexas.com

San Antonio: http://www.visitsanantonio.com

Austin: http://www.austintexas.org/

Abilene: www.abilene.com/visitors

Amarillo: http://www.visitamarillotx.com

Waco: http://www.wacocvb.com/

Truly Bizarre Events, Unexplained Phenomena, and Notorious Texans

Texas Bigfoot Research Center, Dallas, Texas: www.texas-bigfoot.com

Ghost capital of Texas: www.OldTownSpring.com

Politics, Transportation, and Military Tales

The Reverend Cannon's Ezekiel Airship: www.pittsburgtx-museum.com

Fort Sam Houston: http://fshtx.army.mil

Palo Alto Battlefield National Historic Site: www.nps.gov/paal

USS Lexington: www.usslexington.com

Harvey Girls: www.harveyhouses.net

Before "the" War

Alabama-Coushatta Tribe's Web site: www.alabama-coushatta.com

Marfa mystery lights: www.marfalights.com

Brazosport area (where Texas history began): www.brazosport.org

San Jacinto Battleground State Historic Site: www.tpwd.state.tx.us/spdest/findadest/parks/san_jacinto_battleground

Native Americans in Texas: www.texasindians.com

Famous Texans

On U.S. presidents and their First Ladies: www.whitehouse.gov

Black Gold and Cowboy and Rodeo Tales

Texas Cowboy Poetry Gathering (annual competition): http://www.cowboy-poetry.org/news.html

World's First Rodeo (and related information): www.pecostx.com

All things rodeo: www.101wildwestrodeo.com

Spindletop/Gladys City Boomtown: www.spindletop.org

Beaumont (world's first oil boomtown): www.beaumontcvb.org

Religion and Utopian Communities

Eckankar: www.eckankar-texas.org

The Cross of Our Lord Jesus Christ (Groom, Texas): www.crossministries.net

Galveston's Bishop Palace: www.galveston.com/bishopspalace

Sports Stories

Marshall, Texas: http://www.goherd.com

Deep Sea Roundup (Port Aransas): www.deepsearoundup.com

Dallas Cowboys: www.dallascowboys.com

Dallas Cowboys Cheerleaders: www.DallasCowboys.com/cheerleaders

Texas Longhorns: http://www.mackbrown-texasfootball.com/

Wheelers and Dealers

King Ranch: www.king-ranch.com

Gladys' Bakery: http://www.gladysfruitcakes.com/

Flora, Fauna, and Natural Phenomena

Brighter Days Horse Refuge: www.brighterdayshorserefuge.org

Bat Conservational International (Austin): www.batcon.org

McDonald Observatory: www.mcdonaldobservatory.org

Texas State Aquarium: www.texasstateaquarium.org

University of Texas Marine Science Institute: www.utmsi.utexas.edu

Texas Camel Corps: www.texascamelcorps.com

Speech, Food, and Fascinating Cultural Tidbits

Texas Chainsaw Massacre (the three main Web sites for fans): www.texaschainsawmassacre.net, www.txfearfest.com, and http://www.tobehooper.com/.

Clute's Great Texas Mosquito Festival: www.mosquitofestival.com

Burton Cotton Gin & Museum: www.cottonginmuseum.org

Spamarama: www.spamarama.com

Unusual Grave and Burial-Site Stories

New London School explosion: www.nlse.org

Texas City 1947 explosion: http://www.local1259iaff.org/disaster.html

Lighthouse and Coastal Stories

Texas Maritime Museum, Rockport: www.texasmaritime-museum.org

Forbidden Gardens, Katy: www.forbidden-gardens.com

Port Aransas: www.portaransas.org

Sea Turtle, Inc.: www.seaturtleinc.com

www.Dallascvb.com

www.Galveston.com.

INDEX